TABLE OF CONTENTS

EXECUTIVE SUMMARY

NYC 2040: Housing the Next One Million New Yorkers builds upon the observations that NYC's population is growing at a slower pace than many public and private analysts and plans had projected. Based on current growth patterns, it is unlikely that NYC will reach an additional one million residents until 2040. A central finding of this report is that—even at this slower rate of growth—NYC has arguably not developed the zoning capacity and market mechanisms to house the anticipated additional population. More specifically, NYC currently does not have the capacity to produce the same level of product diversity as there is corresponding population diversity. The consequence of this lack of zoned and market capacity is an amplification of the existing affordable housing crisis. Left unabated, the affordability crisis will further impede the efforts to attract and retain a diverse workforce which is critical to NYC's long term urban competiveness.

An analysis of properties which are capable and feasible for redevelopment indicates that, of the one million new New Yorkers anticipated by 2040, approximately 70% of the new residents could be accommodated through infill development within the existing fabric of NYC's diverse neighborhoods. This may be surprising in light of the extraordinary amount of excess zoned floor area (FAR) ostensibly available for redevelopment. The report's analysis indicates that the majority of this surplus FAR is not developable because the floor area is "landlocked." Qualitatively, this could be for a combination of reasons, including: (i) lots are too small for lawful development; (ii) existing buildings have no economic incentive to be recapitalized so as to capture small of amounts of excess FAR; (iii) ambiguous application of historic landmarking; (iv) environmental contamination; and, (v) a lack of market fundamentals and depth.

For the estimated remaining 30% of the projected new population, the report tests the hypothesis that there are certain hyper-urban zones with excess infrastructural capacity that can handle the balance of the new residents. The resulting simulations demonstrate the capacity and feasibility of hyper-urbanized developments where the distance between housing, employment and consumption can be optimized. Many of these tested zones make-up the city's existing or potential "megaprojects." Many of these are well known, such as Hudson Yards and Atlantic Yards. However, as this report discusses, our existing planned megaprojects will house only a fraction of the projected demand. The report evaluates a variety of potential zones in NYC which are potentially available for hyper-urban development. While a few large sites remain in Manhattan, the majority of these zones are in western Brooklyn and Queens, as well as southern portions of the Bronx. While rich in low-density developable land, Staten Island largely does not have the requisite capacity to support the transit-oriented development this report is testing.

With a few geographic exceptions, these zones represent a new economic continuum up the East River which has the potential to rival its own history in terms of urbanization and productivity. The majority of these hyper-urban zones are on or near the water in formerly industrial districts, indicating that despite the impacts of climate change, NYC can and must build resilient, high-density waterfront development. While this vulnerability is an immediate concern in a post-Sandy era, the long-term question with regard to waterfront development is not whether to build it but how to build it.

This report also raises some fundamental questions about social equity and the extent to which consumers and citizens are bifurcated into classes of users and financiers of infrastructure. Hurricane Sandy exposed the inequality and vulnerability of housing in NYC and the extent to which housing is a core social infrastructure that transcends its function as shelter. Manhattan by itself has inequity levels that rival sub-Saharan Africa. While this is at one level indicative of a city that attracts impoverished strivers from the world over seeking a better life for themselves and their children, it also indicates a dire situation in terms of affordable housing.

High-density, mixed-income, transit-oriented development is the key to solving the problems of uneven prosperity, environmental degradation and unequal opportunity. Development is also fundamentally about redevelopment, as historic preservation also plays a critical role in shaping the identity of our city and as a mechanism for the preservation of valuable affordable housing. The analysis made herein allows one to make the argument that simultaneous infrastructure investments that double down on new opportunities for all New Yorkers have the potential to recapture those investment in ways which speak to a stronger fiscal state and a high quality of living for all New Yorkers.

NYC must use hyper-urban development, to build the transit, education, recreation, workplace and community infrastructure that the city will need to support the new housing called for in this report. If NYC does not take these actions, this projected population growth could instead go either to our suburbs or to other regions with which the city competes with nationally and internationally. This flight of people and capital would result in a significant loss of municipal tax base, an increased regional carbon footprint, a loss of affordable housing investment and the potential for a perilous downward cycle for NYC by mid-century. The urgency of all New Yorkers who seek affordable, safe and decent shelter is the current reality. This report tests and advocates for the proposition that hyper-density offers one of several strategies which together define a broader policy for the maintenance of the long-term integrity of NYC's housing stock.

NEW YORK CITY STUDY ZONES

WILLET'S POINT

SHERIDAN EXPRESSWAY

QUEENS BOULEVARD

SOUTH CONCOURSE

125TH STREET

LONG ISLAND CITY

WEST SIDE

SEWARD PARK

DOWNTOWN MANHATTAN

RED HOOK

ST. GEORGE / STAPLETON

BROOKLYN WATERFRONT

DOWNTOWN BROOKLYN

ATLANTIC YARDS

ATLANTIC AVENUE

I. INTRODUCTION

This report examines the spatial and market implications of housing the next one million New Yorkers between now and the year 2040. The intent of this report is to examine and represent a series of feasible scenarios under which pre-selected areas ("Zones") of New York City ("NYC") can sustainably accommodate, through increased levels of density and intensity, a disproportionate amount of the projected population growth and corresponding growth of the built environment. The core methodology for measuring this simulated growth is a combination of conventional geographic information system ("GIS") techniques and experimental computer simulated development studies which measure spatial, financial and experiential sensitivities at a variety of scales from the street to the district. The core intent of this report is to give policy makers and communities a more precise sense of the scale and orders of magnitudes facing the city's long-term housing needs.

HYPOTHESIS

The initial premise of this experimental research is that — given the likelihood of the realization of the projected population growth of one million New Yorkers (9,200,000) — there are spatial and financial impacts which have been undefined or unappreciated to-date and are of such a magnitude that an examination of either facet in isolation does not appreciate the totality of options available for guiding and managing said growth. The core predicate of the hypothesis is that there are markets (i.e., projected demand in tandem with existing land and future building supplies) which have yet to be identified that will drive the allocation of public and private resources for the provision of housing. The hypothesis is that some range of the percentage capture—to be defined—of the next one million New Yorkers can be concentrated in discernible zones of higher density so as to maximize the efficient delivery and consumption of urban services. This report argues that there is gap between planned and actual housing capacity of approximately 300,000 people. The testable component of this hypothesis is that there are certain physically discernible zones in NYC which have the physical, financial and human capacities which qualify said zones for a greater allocation of the project growth. By simulating the aforementioned market demand, the capacity and the feasibility of the study zones can be tested against a complex array of ordered and weighted priorities by and between a variety of actors and stakeholders.

The relevance of this hypothesis is that the provision and quality of housing is increasingly becoming a major determinate for global urban competitiveness.[1] Therefore, if NYC desires to be competitive for the likes of attracting global capital with London, Tokyo, Hong Kong and Shanghai, then these long-term simulations are an invaluable exercise for developing policy for public actors and strategic investment practices for private actors. By visualizing the generative outcomes of various scenarios, the applications of this research are as closely linked in conceptual terms to the field of growth management as it is to the more formal conventions of design and development analysis. For all actors involved, the goal is to manage growth in such a way that we can quantitatively "pay" for the requisite physical infrastructure and development, at the same time we can qualitatively advance the standard of living for all New Yorkers. This is especially true for those in the subject research zones which would ostensibly face greater challenges from increased density and intensity of use.

DEMOGRAPHIC PROJECTIONS

Any discussion as to the projected population growth of NYC should be tempered by understanding the highly contentious implications that such projections have on the allocation of federal, state and city resources. Nowhere was this contention more evident than in the city's unsuccessful challenge of the results of the 2010 census, which the city claimed under-counted NYC's population by roughly 80,000 residents—particularly in Queens and Brooklyn where net-migration among foreign born residents is especially difficult to accurately count.[2] According to the Brookings Institution, each undercounted NYC resident means a loss of approximately $2,117 in corresponding annual revenue from the federal government.[3] When you update this 2008 figure to account for consumer inflation (not inflation in government spending) the 2012 number is closer to $2,400, which would mean a net phantom loss to the city of close to $2.2 billion between now and the next census. With time this decade long deficit will double by 2040 to $4.4 billion with each under counted resident costing NYC $4,791 a year.

---

1. *See, Global Power City Index*, Institute for Urban Strategies, The Mori Memorial Foundation (2011)(Figure 4.1 cites NYC as the top globally competitive city; however, NYC's position is endangered given the relatively low scoring for livability compared to its competitors (in order of ranking) London, Paris, Tokyo and Singapore; *see also, Hot Spots: Benchmarking Global City Competitiveness*, Economist Intelligence Unit (2012)(NYC ranks #1 in Overall Score, but ranks #24 in Physical Capacity which impacts, as a matter of methodological implication, NYC's relatively low #18 ranking for Human Capacity).

2. *Population: 2010 Census Challenge*, Department of City Planning, New York City (April 1, 2012).

3. Metropolitan Policy Program, *Counting for Dollars: New York, NY-NJ-PA*, Brookings Institution (2008).

Another perspective on population growth is the loss of population from New York City to the surrounding suburbs, although this trend in favor of suburban growth sharply reversed course in the 2011 population estimates with NYC growing an estimated 33% faster than its metropolitan area.[4] This can most likely be attributable to net job creation within the city. However, the long-term projections are not nearly as favorable. For instance, the New York metropolitan area grew in the 2010 census from 18,323,000 to 18,897,000, or about three percent (3%). While the City of New York and the inner-ring suburbs grew by roughly two percent (2%), the outer ring suburbs grew by a little over six percent (6%).[5] This explains in part why the Census Bureau's 2010 projection was off by roughly a quarter of million people. While little empirical research has been completed to explain the recent suburbanization in New York, consumer preference factors, which balance increased transportation costs with lower housing costs, provide at least a partial explanation. However, given the increased sensitivity of consumer expenditures to transportation costs—namely higher gas prices—the long-term trend in favor of greater urbanization is promising.[6]

A core assumption of this report is that capturing population growth in an urban environment is critical for maintaining the long-term provision of services in the face of global competition by and between cities. Despite the comparatively sluggish growth over the last decade, the prospect of the next one million New Yorkers is not so much a rhetorical device as it is a moderately plausible proposition between now and 2040. Just prior to the last census, the consensus was that NYC would hit the one million additional resident mark somewhere between 2030 and 2035.[7]

To understand the implications of these projections, it is useful to look at the rates of growth since 1990. From 1990 to 2000, the city grew at a decade long growth rate of 8.56%. At this rate of growth, the city would reach the one million mark prior to 2030, with an additional population of two million, three hundred thousand (2.3 million) by 2040. From 2000 to 2010, the city grew at a much slower rate of approximately 2.87%, which means that—at the same trajectory of growth on a census by census basis—the city would only add 730,000 residents by 2040. However, if the

4. Sam Roberts, *New York Led Country in Population Growth Since 2010 Census*, NY TIMES (June 28, 2012).

5. Wendell Cox, *The Accelerating Suburbanization of New York*, NEW GEOGRAPHY (March 29, 2011).

6. *See generally*, Todd Litman, *Where We Want to Be: Home Location Preferences and Their Implications for Smart Growth*, Victoria Transport Policy Institute (July 26, 2012).

7. *See, New York City Population Projections Age/Sex & Borough 2000-2030 Report*, NYC Department of City Planning (December 2006); *A Shared Vision for Shared Future: Regional Transportation Plan*, Metropolitan Transportation Council (2010); It should be noted that the start of the one million additional resident mark was the year 2000, whereas for the purposes of this report the year has been updated to the year 2010.

basis—the city would only add 730,000 residents by 2040. However, if the pace of population growth is just 3.89% then the city will reach the one million mark by 2040.[8] This represents a modest 35.54% rate of growth over and above the previous census's rate of growth. Without applying any notion of probability to the outcome, this report assumes that the 3.89% is a reasonable rate of growth given the long-run trajectory of the city as a center for job creation and relatively economic stability.[9]

SPATIAL CAPACITY

One of the core tasks of this report is to try and understand the space requirements for housing these new one million New Yorkers. With a population density of 27,243 people per square mile, this means that for every 1% of growth in the census between now and 2040, NYC will naturally increase in density by 3%. As a result, these new New Yorkers would increase the natural population density in NYC by 12.1%. While density measured in terms of population over land area is perhaps the least sophisticated measure of density, it is instructive of the scale of the challenge that faces both regulators and developers as the built environment in NYC further densifies to match the population growth.[10]

NYC is much more suburban than many observers would otherwise suspect with 27% of its housing units in single family structures of one or two units.[11] With the exception of Staten Island, NYC simply has very little land left to promote the continued development of single family housing in any meaningful way so as to capture the increased population growth cited herein. This broad assertion is qualitatively grounded by the fact that areas which could handle additional single family construction are often located a significant distance from existing mass transit infrastructure. As a consequence—and as more specifically discussed in the methodology section below—this report assumes that the entirety of the population growth will be captured in multi-family dwellings at an urban scale. In addition to the spatial requirements of housing the additional population, this report also includes a calculation of the requisite retail square footage necessary to service this new population. It also includes some office space allocations in select zones which already have some locational preferences for commuters and planners alike.

---

8. Based on authors' calculations from U.S. Census Bureau data.

9. *See*, Long Term Occupational Employment Projections (2008-2018), Regional Data: New York City, New York State Department of Labor (2008) (citing a long-term growth rate of jobs at 3.8%); *see also*, Press Release, New York State Department of Labor (November 15, 2012)(citing an annual job growth rate of 2.9%).

10. *See generally*, Meta Berghauser Pont and Per Haupt, SPACEMATRIX: SPACE, DENSITY AND URBAN FORM (NAI Publishers 2010).

11. *Distribution of Occupied and Vacant Available Units by Building Size*, New York City Housing and Vacancy Survey, New York City Department of Housing Preservation and Development (2008).

One question that predisposes the analysis hereof relates to the existing capacity of NYC to handle the additional population as-of-right. As Table 1 notes, the existing as-of-right residential gross developable floor area is 1,645,064,599, which translates to 743,113 units for 1,924,663 people. However, this is a somewhat superficial analysis as it assumes that all of the density (as measured as, "FAR") allocated to mixed-use and vacant property would be allocated for residential uses or is otherwise fit for development. By isolating residential and vacant land categories independently, they account for a population capacity of 1,681,079 and 859,049, respectively. Again this is a somewhat superficial analysis to the extent that additional FAR on-top of a functioning building whose owners are not economically incentivized to redevelop is useless in terms of advancing the production of new units.

Given the relative inflexibility to transfer commodified units of FAR, and/or the relative proliferation of landmark protection, it is unlikely that so much density could make its way to the market in either newly constructed or renovated space. Likewise, it is questionable to the extent to which existing vacant property can be developed given the fact that vacant lots often have environmental problems; are used as community spaces; and/or, are otherwise challenged by physical or economic limiting characteristics. With an average vacant lot size of less than 1,500 square feet, perhaps one of the single most significant reasons that hinder the development of vacant lots is that their size is very often too small for financially feasible development.[12]   As such, aggregate excess FAR on small lots may produce noise which is not helpful to the underlying analysis.

As discussed in more detail below, this report utilizes a GIS based soft-site index which identifies sites which are more or less suitable for development ("Development Index"). The index operates as a filter to sort out lots which will most likely not or cannot be the site of future housing development. An application of the Development Index city-wide shows a much lower capacity to handle additional housing at just 727,021 people—with a heavy reliance on vacant properties at 569,423 and just 30,082 for residential properties. To give some perspective on the scale of these numbers, the top five major long-term real estate megaprojects in NYC (Hudson Yards, Atlantic Yards, Willets Point, Hunters Point and Seward Park) account for just 37,351,000 residential square feet for an estimated 78,342 people.[13] This presently planned megaproject capacity

---

12. *See*, David A. King and Jesse M. Keenan, *Understanding the Role of Parking Lots in Urban Redevelopment*, Center for Urban Real Estate, Columbia University (July 2012).

13. New York City Economic Development Corporation; Empire State Development Corporation; New York City Department of City Planning; The Related Companies.

TABLE 1: RESIDENTIAL DEVELOPMENT CAPACITY

	AS-OF-RIGHT SQ. FT.	AS-OF-RIGHT HOUSEHOLDS	AS-OF-RIGHT POPULATION	DEVELOPMENT INDEX (DI) > 0.6 SQ. FT.	DI HOUSEHOLDS	DI POPULATION	DIFFERENCE (SQ. FT.)	DIFFERENCE (%)
MANHATTAN								
Total Housing Avail GFA	314,236,727	205,305	531,739	67,160,718	43,879	113,647	247,076,009	78.63%
Total Available Resi	175,690,117	114,786	297,296	10,643,830	6,954	18,011	165,046,287	93.94%
Total Available Mixed	72,502,833	47,369	122,686	3,602,264	2,354	6,096	68,900,569	95.03%
Total Available Vacant	66,043,776	43,149	111,757	52,914,624	34,571	89,540	13,129,152	19.88%
BRONX								
Total Housing Avail GFA	244,496,548	159,740	413,727	25,231,586	16,485	42,696	219,264,962	89.68%
Total Available Resi	175,272,276	114,513	296,589	6,002	4	10	175,266,274	100%
Total Available Mixed	15,796,882	10,321	26,731	0	0	0	15,796,882	100%
Total Available Vacant	53,427,390	34,906	90,408	25,225,584	16,481	42,686	28,201,806	52.79%
QUEENS								
Total Housing Avail GFA	380,323,683	248,482	643,568	62,467,521	40,813	105,705	317,856,162	83.58%
Total Available Resi	267,515,066	174,779	452,678	5,569,431	3,639	9,424	261,945,635	97.92%
Total Available Mixed	17,590,295	11,493	29,766	217,315	142	368	17,372,980	98.76%
Total Available Vacant	95,218,323	62,210	161,125	56,680,775	37,032	95,913	38,537,548	40.47%
BROOKLYN								
Total Housing Avail GFA	415,398,155	271,398	702,920	51,997,102	33,972	87,987	363,401,053	87.48%
Total Available Resi	279,855,836	182,842	473,561	170,216	111	288	279,685,620	99.94%
Total Available Mixed	35,755,967	23,361	60,505	0	0	0	35,755,967	100%
Total Available Vacant	99,786,352	65,195	168,854	51,826,886	33,861	87,699	47,959,466	48.06%
STATEN ISLAND								
Total Housing Avail GFA	290,609,485	189,868	491,758	222,784,053	145,555	376,986	67,825,432	23.34%
Total Available Resi	95,118,336	62,145	160,955	1,387,717	907	2,348	93,730,619	98.54%
Total Available Mixed	2,302,514	1,504	3,896	126,479	83	214	2,176,035	94.51%
Total Available Vacant	193,188,636	126,219	326,906	149,858,659	97,909	253,585	43,329,977	22.43%
NYC TOTAL								
Total Housing Avail GFA	1,645,064,599	743,113	1,924,663	429,640,980	280,703	727,021	1,215,423,619	73.88%
Total Available Resi	993,451,630	649,065	1,681,079	17,777,196	11,615	30,082	975,674,434	98.21%
Total Available Mixed	143,948,492	94,048	243,584	3,946,058	2,578	6,677	140,002,434	97.26%
Total Available Vacant	507,664,477	331,679	859,049	336,506,528	219,854	569,423	171,157,949	33.71%

*Average Houshold Size (2.59) / 1,301 Sq. Ft. Per Unit

6

represents just 7.8% of the projected need of 386,137 units for one million people.

To give a greater sense of scale as to how many units will be needed, 386,137 is a little more than two times (2x) all of the housing units presently in Staten Island.[14] Over the last eleven years, NYC averaged about 18,018 units a year coming on-line.[15] At this rate, there would be ample supply of units to accommodate the expected growth.[16] However, the boom years of 2005-2009 which averaged 20,928 units skewed the long-run average which is closer to 7,000 units a year over the last 35 years. In 2011, the city issued just 6,430 certificates of occupancy for new housing units. At this present rate of growth, the city would need to double its annual housing production in order to meet the projected demand between now and 2040. Assuming that there would be at least three real estate cycles between now and then, it is not improbable to assume that the present rate of growth would increase on average through various boom cycles. The question remains as to what extent production will keep up with demand given that NYC has technically been in a housing "emergency" for the past 40 years with a current vacancy rate of just 3.12%.[17] At 305,000 units, almost as many homes were impacted by Hurricane Sandy as is the subject of this report.[18] There is little doubt that this natural and human disaster will alter the spatial development of NYC's housing stock for at least the next decade.

The most significant limitation to looking at these numbers in their two dimensions is that one overlooks the importance of the three dimensional distribution of the square footage.[19] As demonstrated in each borough's Available FAR and Development Index maps, the distribution of relative available FAR is highly asymmetrical and largely follows the patterns of industrialization which stich together various neighborhoods. It should be noted that the results of Development Index maps illustrate

---

14. N=175,077; Moon Wha Lee, *Selected Initial Finding of the 2011 New York City Housing and Vacancy Survey*, New York City Department of Housing Preservation and Development (February 9, 2012) at Table 2.

15. Units Issued New Certificates of Occupancy. It should be noted that new certificates of occupancy are issued for both new construction and renovated units, which can account for up to 25% of the total number; *State of the City's Housing & Neighborhoods*, Furman Center for Real Estate and Urban Policy, New York University (2001-2011).

16. *Id.*, N=504,512 Units by 2040.

17. Elizabeth A. Harris, *Decades-Old Housing 'Emergency' Continues, and So Does Rent Regulation*, NY TIMES (March 26, 2012).

18. *Governor Cuomo Holds Meeting with New York's Congressional Delegation, Mayor Bloomberg and Regional County Executives to Review Damage Assessment for the State in the Wake of Hurricane Sandy*, Press Release, Governor Andrew M. Cuomo Press Office (November 26, 2012).

19. *See generally*, Andy L. Krause and Christopher Bitter, *Spatial Econometrics, Land Values and Sustainability: Trends in Real Estate Valuation Research*, CITIES (July 2012).

a remarkable consistency with existing sub-market activity. This report assumes that roughly 70% of the subject growth will be absorbed in a systematic process of infill development. This percentage is based on a rounded numerator of the city-wide Development Index capacity analysis of 727,021. The remaining 30% of one million new New Yorkers are allocated to the subject zones which in the aggregate measure 7.11 square miles—or, just 1.52% of NYC's land area. The existing market trends in favor of broader concentration of development along the waterfront may be thwarted in the wake of Sandy and may accelerate upland infill over concentrated peripheral density. As discussed further, this report reinforces the trend of urbanization along the waterfront but at a cost—the cost of the requisite infrastructure to insure the long-term physical integrity of the zones themselves.

VISUALIZING SCALE

This report visualizes the space requirements of the additional population in two different scenarios. The first scenario tests the hypothesis that the selected zones can in the aggregate handle 30% of new population—or, approximately 300,000 people. This number represents the rounded difference between the Development Index maximum FAR capacity and the projected spatial requirements of one million New Yorkers. Under this scenario, the population is allocated to a weighted distribution by borough and zone based on the existing patternization and density of each respective zone. While the first scenario ("Scenario #1") is an essentially inductive process, the second scenario ("Scenario #2") is deductive as the allocation of space is hypothetically stretched to the physical limits of each zone so as to test the upward bounds of respective zone's capacity to physically and qualitatively handle extreme levels of density.

Therefore, while the first scenario tests a rational allocation of population so that the sum of the projected population equals approximately 300,000 people, the second scenario will exceed an aggregate of 300,000 people as each individual zone will be physically maximized irrespective of any given zone's relationship to the other zones and the rest of the city. The results represented in this report from one model iteration calculate a Scenario #2 simulation capacity at 472,391 people.[20] The purpose of

---

20. The actual total aggregate population under the simulations in Scenario #1 is 278,254 compared to the allocated projected of 293,940, which included Zones and megaprojects. The difference can be attributable to some lots qualifying under the Development Index but otherwise having a disqualifying characteristic that required manual exclusion.

this second scenario is two-fold. First, it provides an upper boundary from which to test qualitative experiential qualities of density in Scenario #1. Second, it allows for an alternative scenario whereas zones, such as Long Island City, can and probably will handle much greater levels of density than is allocated under Scenario #1. Third, it provides an alternative scenario wherein some or all of the developments in other zones under Scenario #1 are unrealized and/or realized infill development in non-zones is less than 70% of the captured population.

While many may find the simulated hyper density of the second scenario objectionable, the exercise is meant to stimulate an informed dialogue about the costs and impacts of density—and not just the subjective experience of radically changing one neighborhood into a zone of higher density. To this end, the visualization of both scenarios represents simulations and not normative expressions for what the urban fabric should look like. The tools developed in this project are intended to be utilized iteratively in the context of managing a design and development workflow. As such, Scenario #2 as represented is just one of scores of plausible scenarios where more or less relative density could be allocated.

II. SCOPE OF RESEARCH

RESEARCH DESIGN & METHODOLOGY

This research is the subject of a mixed-methods approach which combines qualitative interviews and field work, quantitative and qualitative GIS analysis and experimental computational design. The core mechanics of the computational design are grounded in the linkage between Excel, Rhino/Grasshopper, ArcGIS and Galapagos Evolutionary Solver software programs, as noted more particularly in Diagram 1. The research design itself is experimental to the extent that program inputs and outputs are iteratively measured and inferentially defined to achieve validation and calibration of both.[21] Although, on some level, the validation of the results (i.e., resulting urban massing configurations) are subject to the subjective interpretation of the reader who will draw their own conclusions as to the validation of any given result. The entire design is based on a fixed treatment structure of the sampling units (zones) based on a simulation of market behavior (static supply and demand).[22] In this case, the simulation itself is of the assumed behavior of a constant net growth in population and corresponding housing demand. Therefore, the control variable is demand and the dependent variables are the volumetric and locational characteristics of the resulting real estate development. This combination of methods and techniques is relevant beyond the scope of this report for its potential to be integrated into Building Information Modeling software (BIM) and its corresponding workflow. This is in contrast to many simulation programs such as UrbanSim and AnyLogic, which are many times more sophisticated but are not integrated in formal architectural design, development and construction processes.

The first step in the research process was to identify the specific boundaries of each zone which are the subject of the hypothesis. Preliminary boundaries were drawn up at a variety of scales to cover neighborhoods, districts and projects in all 5 boroughs. Their initial list of 32 zones were narrowed down to 15 zones over the course of 2 separate focus groups which looked a variety of un-weighted qualitative and quantitative factors. While some factors such as proximate distance to mass transit and market rates were pre-identified prior to the focus group, other factors such as measuring the momentum of real estate sub-markets by evaluating industry press and public process initiatives materialized through the focus

---

21. Henri H. Achten, *Experiment Design Methods: A Review*, 7 INT.'L J. OF ARCHITECTURAL COMPUTING 4, 505 (2010); *see also*, Nigel Cross, ENGINEERING DESIGN METHODS: STRATEGIES FOR PRODUCT DESIGN (Wiley 2000).

22. *See generally*, John Chris Jones, DESIGN METHODS: SEEDS OF HUMAN FUTURES (Wiley 1981).

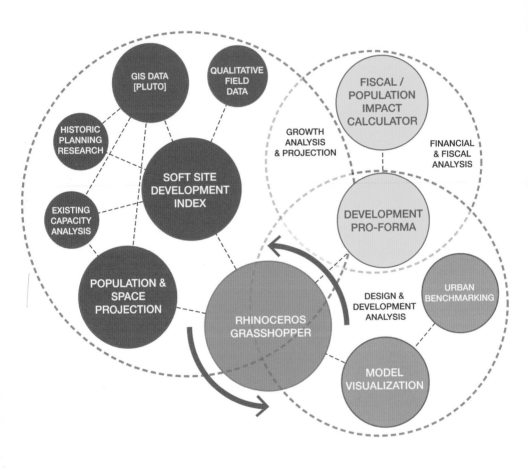

group exercises. A final preliminary step included extensive mapping in GIS of various housing, density and mass transit metrics to further understand the systematic relationship of any given zone to the rest of the city. Utilizing these GIS maps and other primary and secondary sources, the focus groups, which were made up of internal CURE affiliated researchers and external private participants, rationally filtered through the zones through a logical process that began to weight factors through the development of stated priorities (i.e., mass transit, market transparency and intensity, etc...).

Following the first round of filtering, historical research was done on each subject zone and/or areas surrounding the zones. Utilizing the extensive catalog at Avery Library, the following materials were sourced going back to the turn of the 20th century: (i) public or private development plans whether, executed or conceptual; (ii) public actions, such as re-zonings and bond issuances; (iii) market reports; (iv) social and public health impact studies; and, (v) community planning memorandum and position texts. In some cases, interviews were conducted with planning officials, community board planners and community organizations to fill-in the gaps so as to create a continuous narrative of the history of the development of each zone. The researchers felt that this historical method was critical to understanding the long-term needs and ambitions of each zone. In many zones, a consistent theme or a consistent area was recognized or identified only after several generations of planning and envisioning. This historical method was viewed as a necessary intermediate step to mitigate certain biases that come along with the top down perspective which drove the balance of the process. Following the final selection of the final zones, researchers began the process of walking almost every street within each zone documenting environmental and social conditions which were previously undocumented by the previous empirical research.

DEVELOPMENT INDEX

The next step was to develop a Development Index. The initial design conceptualized an index based on a statistically significant sample of transaction data which would shed light on property characteristics that could identify the property as being more or less subject to development in its current state. Initial test samples proved inconclusive for two primary reasons. First, the data recorded in each transaction did not shed light as to the identity or the future intent of the parties involved. While some properties could easily be researched, many more were cloaked, often intentionally, in anonymity. It became clear that relying on well documented developments simply undermined the notion of a random and representative sample. Second, unrecorded data relating to the motivations and value attributed to specific property characteristics were largely unavailable. Focused case studies of projects could have shed light on these characteristics but not to the extent that the data would have been generalizable across all five boroughs or even within borough specific sub-markets.

As the quantitative method came up short, it was decided that a Development Index could be equally as defensible through a qualitative ranking of ordered characteristics found in the city's Pluto GIS files. As described in Appendix Table 1, the method was to assigned a numeric value of 0 through 5 to combined tax lot and building characteristics data sub-categorized by zoning code, building class, land use code and year built. The sum was equally weighted by sub-category and indexed to 1.0. A casual reading of Appendix Table 1 suggests a series of logical scenarios which justify some of the weighting components. For example, the index would preference for development: (i) a manufacturing building built before 1900 (that was not landmarked) over a multi-family building built in 2000; (ii) a parking lot over a park; (iii) a warehouse built in the 1930s over an office building built in the 1980s; (iv) a rental multi-family building over a cooperative or condo building; or, even (iv) a single family house over a multifamily building of the same year, etc.... The least refined step in the process is the random assignment of equal intervals between the characteristics of the sub-categories. The development of a soft-site GIS index could benefit from future research utilizing large transactional data sets to test the validity and/or establish a calibration of the weighting of existing characteristics and/or yet-to-be discovered characteristics. Very similar hedonic techniques could significantly contribute to the idea of valuing "good" design and/or justifying certain historic landmarking measures.

GRASSHOPPER / RHINO SCRIPTING

The next steps in the "calibration" of the Development Index came in two steps: (i) spatial distribution modeling; and, (ii) conventional on-the-ground real estate due diligence. It was at this stage that the calculations were undertaken by utilizing excel linked to GIS via custom coding of scripts operating within Grasshopper, which is a generative modeling tool and algorithm editor running within the Rhino design platform. The initial step was to develop a series of rules which preferenced the allocation of density (i.e., future housing units) within blocks, streets and districts within the zone. This was done by identifying various services, amenities and urban characteristics which could have a spatialized range of influence or level of service. For instance, properties are biased in quarter mile increments from subway and bus stops—with a greater influence assigned to subway over bus stops, for instance. Similar rules apply to parks, retail zones, schools, or work inversely to negative tractor points such as busy highways, polluted sites and active industrial uses.

In addition to the modeled spatial influences, geometric calculations were made on each lot to establish minimum massing thresholds by and between programs and typologies.[23] Larger lots which can offer greater levered returns through economy of scale are biased against small lots which must meet the minimum developable capacity requirements by allocated program. The intra-block dynamics were modeled so that both lots and blocks have separated scores wherein the lot-score is partially dependent on the block-score. As a general rule, larger lots are developed first. However, high scoring smaller lots in high scoring blocks (with disproportionate amounts of FAR) were then grouped into a second round of allocated lots which were assigned one of several land banking functions. The algorithm first merged contiguous properties and then combined FAR on intra-block lots to allocate a greater amount of density in small number of developments. This had the effect of increasing verticality in the resulting form. All resulting building massing and programs attempt to fit within proscribed lawful envelopes and uses, but a true lawful massing contingent on a multitude of various special use districts and urban design best practices is some years away. Likewise, building orientation relative to environmental conditions, line of sight, and other site specific optimization criteria are currently under development and were not utilized in this report.

These combinations of FAR are premised on the novel idea of 'Cap and Trade Zoning' wherein FAR can be transacted by and between non-contiguous lots.[24] The unapplied component of this theoretical model is that both density and uses can be transacted. As noted in Diagram 2, the mechanics of the process are that all of the property owners are brought up and down to a constant ceiling of density. For example, if one lot has positive 7.5 FAR and another lot has negative .5 FAR, then the ceiling would adjust both properties to 4.0 FAR. This has the effect of being both a down- and an up-zoning. The idea would to then create a cap FAR, which, as per the example, would be something closer to 10 FAR. In order to get the additional FAR for any one project between 4.0 and 10 FAR, the developer would then need to buy auctioned FAR

---

23. While housing dominates the modeled program, retail and office requirements are modeled in at various multiples depending on the borough per capita averages which range from 10-50 square feet per transient and permanent resident to 100-133 square feet per worker.

24. Based on the authors' untested hypothesis, which was presented at the *Zoning in the City* conference for NYC in 2011.

within a prescribed district—generally within the same block or several blocks. In order to transact this density, the developer would have to make certain programmatic concessions which meet any given specific public policy goals. With time, costs of the concessions would be priced into the transacted density and presumably the price per zoned FAR foot (and/or land prices) would come down in nominal terms. The real challenge and prospect for future research under this model is to determine what cap and ceiling one selects, as you don't want to oversaturate or under-stimulate market demand. However, as represented in Diagram 3, the spatial result may very well result in a more distributive allocation of density in light of a removal of existing requirement that parties to a transaction be contiguous. However, as applied in this report, the idea of Cap and Trade is merely a rationale for the simulated random grouping of buyers and sellers which otherwise are almost entirely unpredictable when it comes to block by block and lot by lot development.

DIAGRAM 2: COMPARISON OF TRADITIONAL TRANSFERABLE
DEVELOPMEN RIGHTS AND CAP AND TRADE TRANSACTIONS

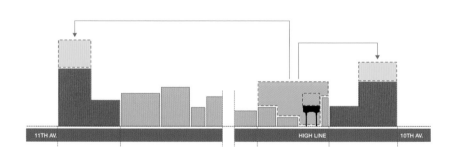

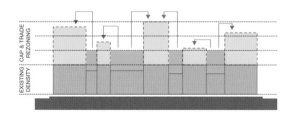

DIAGRAM 3: HYPOTHESIZED SPATIAL DISTRIBUTION OF CAP AND TRADE ZONING

STANDARD DISTRICT ZONING   **CAP & TRADE ZONING**

Once the Development Index included the spatial biasing as incorporated through Grasshopper, the next step was to determine what score a lot must rank within the index to qualify to be developed. After examining the results of a range of cut-off points between .5 and .8, it was decided that .6 was the optimal cut off-point. Part of the justification for this cut-off point can be attributed to the processing limitations of the software in term of the number of buildings being generated and analyzed. Our 100 building modeling threshold proved sufficient to handle all of the subject zones, albeit some larger zones took up a considerable amount of processing capacity. The more considerable factor limiting the score to .6 was that it provided enough scalable lots to handle the allocated density under Scenario #1 without radically requiring the reconfiguration of blocks at the expense of disrupting contextual scale. The distribution of the indexed scores tended to drop off considerably above .60 with 96.7% of the sample scoring below .65. Despite the quantitative metrics assigned to the indexed score, the final cut-off score was ultimately measured by qualitative determinants relating to feasibility, contextual scale and saturation.

Second, preliminary results were subsampled and actual site visits were undertaken. Prior to the site visits, real estate due diligence tasks including title research and permit history were undertaken for the selected to-be-developed lots. In almost every sample, the selected lots were feasible for development in terms of physical properties and locational qualities—irrespective of the actual motivations of the owners of the property. However, some lots developed in this report have already been built on since the start of this research project or may otherwise not be developable for reasons unknown to the researchers. In certain limited cases, lots with architecturally significant and un-landmarked buildings were selected by the model and unselected manually upon further due diligence.

The capturing of the dynamic between the scale of the building and the market programmatic diversity necessary to support the project finance requirements over the denominator of the land price is as much of an art as it is a science in the practice of development. Much of this dynamic is a function of land prices which can vary greatly by zone and which are dependent on existing zoned capacity. To simulate the proper scale of the building so as to represent a viable economic investment decision, various rules were written for define minimum thresholds for building sizes and programs. For instance, a 10,000 square foot lot with 90,000 square feet of FAR may be appropriate for Atlantic Avenue but not for Lower Manhattan.

UNIT / HOUSEHOLD SIZE PROJECTIONS

With the lots and size of the intervening buildings defined by zone, the question then turned to how much space does it take to house approximately 300,000 people in the context of the stated assumed levels of density? The principle calculations for housing space allocations were based on the 2011 results of the Citizens Housing & Planning Council study of the 2010 American Community Survey.[25] As noted in Table 2, each household was deconstructed into various types ranging from nuclear family to shared households with unrelated persons. The percentage allocations were then multiplied by either: (i) average household size (n=2.59): (ii) average family size (n=3.32); (iii) single occupancy (n=1.0); or, (iv) double occupancy (couples with no children; n=2.0), depending on the composition of the household by the terms of the subcategory. To calculate average unit size, the adjusted household size was multiplied by the average size per person, which is close to 450 square feet. This average was determined by aggregating Manhattan residential density and population and netting out vacancy rates, unoccupied unit rate and a loss-factor of 15%. Manhattan was used so as to reinforce the testing of the hypothesis of the application of relative hyper density. As discussed later, Manhattan also provides the baseline from which the urban benchmarking analysis was made. The city-wide average per person is closer to 700 square feet due to the inclusion of large swaths of single family housing

25. *Making Room*, Citizens Housing & Planning Council (2011).

in the outer boroughs. The resulting adjusted average square feet per person was ultimately calculated at 502 square feet due to the surprisingly large amount (27% of all units) of units being under-occupied by singles and couples. The resulting adjusted average unit size as weighted by and between the various household categories was 1,301 square feet. This number was partially validated as to its range by the stated adjusted average unit size of 1,124 square feet for all of NYC.[26] The average sizes were additionally validated when the average unit size was divided by the adjusted average per square foot per person and the result equaled the exact known average household size in NYC (n=2.59).[27]

Once the space allocations for housing were determined at the scale of the unit and the household, the space was distributed first by borough based on a weighted allocation based on relative population of each borough. Second, the space was then distributed to the subject zones within each borough as measured by an allocation formula which gave equal weighting to each zone's: (i) land area; (ii) proximate population density within a half-mile influence of the zone; and, (iii) existing relative building density. Those zones which contained existing megaprojects, such as West Side Manhattan (Hudson Yards), Willets Point and Atlantic Yards were overridden in the calculations for Scenario #1 and the eliminated zone's allocated density was reallocated within the respective eliminated zone's borough. The two zones not subject to an override were Seward Park and Long Island City. Specific to Seward Park, the

TABLE 2: HOUSEHOLD COMPOSITION / SPACE ALLOCATION PROJECTIONS

	HOUSEHOLD COMPOSITION	HOUSEHOLD / FAMILY SIZE	AVERAGE SIZE PER PERSON	AVERAGE SIZE OF UNIT
17%	Nuclear Family	3.32	450	1,494
22%	Single / Alone	1.00	450	450
10%	Single Under-Occupy (2br or larger)	1.00	900	900
6%	Shared (unrelated roommates)	2.59	450	1,166
20%	Shared (w/family)	3.32	450	1,494
17%	Couples with no children	2.00	450	900
8%	Single Parents	3.32	450	1,494
100%	Total Households			
502	Average Sq. Ft. Per Person			
1,301	Average Sq. Ft. Per Household			
2.59	Average Household Size			

26. *Cities with the Largest Average Home Sizes*, REALTOR MAGAZINE (January 03, 2012).

27. Authors' calculations based on 2010 Census.

Request for Proposal had not yet been issued for the zone at the time of the production of this report and it is uncertain as to the exact scale of the project going forward despite the publicized pending agreement with the Seward Park community. Long Island City was exempted—despite the siting of Hunters Point—due to the widely acknowledged capacity of the zone and all of Long Island City to handle a disproportionate amount of allocated density in the future. Adjacent to Long Island City, Sunnyside Yards was excluded from analysis based on the practical and logistical limitations of the site being a working railyard. An additional excluded megaproject site is the Domino Sugar Refinery development in Brooklyn, which was excluded because of the project's still tentative status as it advances through the public process.

IMPACT ANALYSIS

Once the process to define the amount and location of the density (i.e., future housing development) was determined, the next step was to evaluate both: (i) the financial, fiscal and demographic impacts; and, (ii) the relative physical orientation of the resulting urban fabric. The first set of analyses can be broken down into a conventional real estate pro forma analysis which evaluates each individual simulated building, as well as the aggregations of the entire zone, and a fiscal impact calculator which measures anticipated costs of the infrastructure necessary to support the development and the corresponding sources of revenue derived from the subject simulation. Appendix Table 2 shows the conventional range of assumptions which are being calculated in the automated pro-forma which is linked to real-time geometry.

Specific market metrics for construction, land and sales pricing and market rents vary by borough and by zone and are consistent with rates as measured in the second quarter of 2012. Office rents range from $45 to $120 per square foot and retail rents range from $100 to $2,200. Housing rates range from $20 to $45 per square foot on average for rental units and $500 to $1,200 on average for for-sale units. While many practitioners may cite an average for-sale number closer to $2,200 for new development, it is important to note that by including existing sales in the average this brought the overall average sales price down so as to underwrite a more distributive value calculation which is inclusive of market rate and affordable housing development.[28]

The base year construction costs ranged from $300 to $600 per square foot depending on program, typology and location. For instance, zones such as Long Island City and Downtown Brooklyn accurately reflect construction costs and outer borough revenue projections. This tension is reflected most acutely in low return-on-cost calculations for projects in the Bronx and Staten Island. All cost and revenue streams are inflated annually at a constant rate of 2.5%, which is roughly the non-energy consumer rate of inflation. This is somewhat problematic given the spread between nominal and real rates of inflation and the comparatively greater rate of inflation attributable to energy consumption which increasingly is eroding bottom-line net operating income.[29] Likewise, additional work in modeling marginal cost of the power and transportation infrastructure necessary to support future development would be a tremendous addition to the work in this project.

Unless otherwise noted, the monetized figures represented in this report are in 2012 dollars and do not represent stated rates of return. While the tools developed herein can account for building by building investment return analysis, these returns are not represented in this report. As a default rule, the model accounts for sales in the 10th and 20th year to calculate internal rates of return, net present value, return on equity and the like. However, these numbers are a less than helpful number given the long-term hold strategy that many investor/owners adhere to in the NYC market. Likewise, a consistent default hold period for all building does not result in any aggregate data which is useful to ascertain relative value or fiscal impact. To this end, cap rate valuations are a much better reflection of value than internal rates of return. Aggregate values represented in this report are based on sub-market specific cap rates and sales figures by zone. An additional limitation specific to investment return analysis is that all of the buildings, except for the for-sale products, are assumed to have conventional construction and permanent financing with construction loans equaling 65% of loan-to-cost and permanent loans equaling 80% of loan-to-value. As such, the corresponding debt and equity inputs are of equal constants. For these reasons, investment analysis—which is individually ascertainable by building—is not represented in this report for aggregation of development within each zone. Future model development

---

28. This report was underwritten with a 30% allocation of affordable units/buildings. Community groups often ask for more affordable housing with less overall density. This 'best of both worlds' scenario is increasingly untenable in light of the public misunderstanding of the role economies of scale play in subsidizing and/or offsetting projects costs for affordable housing, which are equal to or marginally less than market rate products. A review of Scenario #1 and #2 per capita Annual and Nonrecurring Impacts generally illustrates the potential underlying cost efficiency of greater density assuming an equal distribution of affordable and market rate housing units for both scenarios. These cost efficiencies narrow with the more office development one allocates, which reinforces the notion that new residents in places like Midtown West will be directly subsidizing the office infrastructure in their underlying rents.

29. See generally, Amy S. Rushing, Joshua D. Kneifel and Barbara C. Lippiatt, *Energy Price Indices and Discount Factors for Life-Cycle Cost Analysis- 2011*, U.S. Department of Energy Federal Energy Management Program, NSTIR-85-3273-26 (September 11, 2011).

could include providing some measure of sensitivity to subordinate finance alternatives and interest rate trajectories. Instead of modeling sensitivity to capital investment choices, resources were focused on exploring the operability and sensitivity of property absorption rates and development phasing.

An intuitive step in understanding the long-run absorption rate is trying to time each of the approximately 3 to 4 cycles in the next 28 years.[30] Because this report is focused on housing with a constant and evenly distributed net population, modeling long-run supply and demand elasticities in NYC is unnecessary. That being said the same straight-line distribution utilized for net new housing demand would not be optimal for office space, where shock from broader economic cycles has a much more sustained lag on supply.[31] Therefore, all of the housing and retail density allocated in either Scenario #1 or Scenario #2 is absorbed in less than 2 years upon issuance of a certificate of occupancy. An additional density allocation rule in Grasshopper allocates density to the largest buildings first and works in reverse order with the previously largest building built having its adjusted square feet spread out over successive years so as to maintain a fairly constant rate of supply as grouped at the size of the most "dense" buildings first. A secondary Grasshopper rule set dictates that successive buildings are grouped by largest site capacity first and concentrated so as to develop contextual sub-districts. It should be noted that while the model has the capacity to sequence the density allocations into discernible development phases, the representations presented in this report are of model outputs in the year 2040.

The flow of information relating to the design (or, contextual massings) and development was then filtered through a final calculator which examines: (i) demographic impacts; and, (ii) fiscal impacts. Fiscal impacts can be broken down into two sub-components. The first component calculates the impact of the development as calculated by marginal unit cost of infrastructure, as identified in Table 3. This infrastructure ranges from associated square footage of public facilities to the increased cost of additional consumption. However, infrastructure consumption is not as always clear cut as per capita seasonally adjusted averages. For instance, each scenario is measured for what its optimal park space should be given the level of density and stated levels of service adopted by city planners. In many cases, the optimal level of service for park space far exceeds the physical capacity of any zone or contiguous

---

30. William C. Wheaton, *Real Estate "Cycles": Some Fundamentals*, 2 REAL ESTATE ECONOMICS 27, 209 (1999).

31. *See generally*, Eduardo Schwartz and Walter N. Torous, *Commercial Office Space: Tests of Real Options Model with Competitive Interactions*, Paper Presented at the American Finance Association Annual Meeting (2004).

district. However, the impact is still calculated pursuit to the logic that the potential revenue could be put back into each zone to advance recreation, public space, education and public health amenities as a substitute for the positive benefits attributable to the conventional open-air park.

TABLE 3: MARGINAL COST OF INFRASTRUCTURE IMPACTS

FACILITY		IMPUTED LEVEL OF SERVICE	UNIT COST	
Parks and Recreation	2.50	Acres Per 1,000 Residents	$105,000	Acre
Police	4.18	Officers Per 1,000 Residents	$87,000	Officer
Fire/Emergency Medical	1.90	Officers Per 1,000 Residents	$100,000	Officer
Water	100.00	Gallons Per Capita Per Day	$5	Gallon
Sewer	75.00	Gallons Per Capita Per Day	$10	Gallon
Stormwater	345.00	Sq. Ft. Per Capita	$33	Sq. Ft.
Public Buildings	0.50	Sq. Ft. Per Capita	$300	Sq. Ft.
Courts and Justice	0.50	Sq. Ft. Per Capita	$500	Sq. Ft.
Libraries	0.50	Sq. Ft. Per Capita	$400	Sq. Ft.
Schools	0.36	Students Per Household	$20,000	Student

The second component calculates the tax revenue generated by the operation of the businesses, residents and properties located within the zone. As identified in Appendix Table 7, the model looks at property taxes (by class), construction materials taxes, sales taxes, hotel room occupancy, commercial rent tax and employment taxes.[32] The revenue streams are measured as either: (i) reoccurring or one-time revenue; or, (ii) city or state. The more complicated employment tax projections are based on the future working population mirroring the same distribution of trades and industries that are represented in our current labor force.[33] Therefore, the model attempts to measure retail, office and other trade workers' salaries who would be utilizing the simulated development. Of course, these numbers do not reflect a net positive income adjustment to the city and state because certain jobs may just be moving from one part of the city to one of the subject zones. An additional qualification on employment metrics relates to the stated construction jobs produced for each zone. These job numbers do not represent a one for one relationship between workers and job projects. In other words, one worker may have

---

32. For a discussion on the inequitable property tax classification of multi-family properties, see, Furman Center for Real Estate and Public Policy, *State of the City's Housing & Neighborhoods* (2011).

33. Bureau of Labor Statistics, New York-New Jersey Information Office, *New York City/New York State: State and Area Employment, Hours and Earnings (Non-Farm)*(2012).

several or many jobs over the course of 28 years depending on skill level and age.

This simplification as to the composition of the workforce would not be acceptable for office space calculations given the increasing trend towards horizontality of work spaces as reflected by a changing workforce. There is little doubt that with the proliferation of a more autonomous workforce which is more akin to project based than firm based work habits will have an impact on long-run office and industrial demand. Therefore, the presumed mismatch in the increasing supply of office towers and the decreasing demand from an increasingly decentralized and horizontal workforce has significant implications for NYC.[34] There is an emerging argument that the pace of change in the knowledge economy as reflected in the workforce is changing faster than the useful life of skyscraper presently being designed. The underlying question is whether the workforce will change in such a way to make large conventional office configurations obsolete prior to the end of their useful life?

These questions have significant implications for NYC given the city's long-term bet on the vertical office typology which is necessary to maintain the economic viability of projects such as Hudson Yards. The argument in favor of this bet has cited the increased obsolescence of the midtown-east office stock, but a proposed up-zoning would essentially double down on the long-term bet. In many ways, the city does not have much of a choice but to double-down given the existing investment in transportation infrastructure which services the area where vertical office buildings exist now. The question then shifts to whether residential conversions of obsolete office towers, such as those in the Financial District, or similar residential programming within the up-zoned midtown-east district is a necessary backstop in the event that the office market becomes over-supplied with both Hudson Yards and the World Trade Center master plan space coming on-line. Pursuant to this worst case scenario, it needs to be determined as a matter of policy whether residential conversion or downgrading to B-class office is a least preferable alternative option. In either event, this report does not specifically address the more nuanced spatial relationship between jobs and housing but for the preference of the concentration of density closest to existing job and transportation centers.

---

34. *See generally*, Charles Levy, Andrew Sissons and Charlotte Holloway, *A Plan for Growth in the Knowledge Economy (U.K.)*, A Knowledge Economy Programmer Paper, The Work Foundation (June 2011); Ali Madanipour, KNOWLEDGE ECONOMY AND THE CITY: SPACES OF KNOWLEDGE (Taylor & Francis Group 2011).

VALUE CAPTURE

While the fiscal impacts relating to future employment are simplified in light of the elusiveness of long-term labor market projections, the more immediate focus was originally on a broad set of fiscal impacts as a means to measure the hypothetical imposition of impact fees. Impact fees being defined as the practice wherein local regulatory bodies require a payment of fees to public entities which are in an amount equal to the approximate proportionate impact of a defined set of externalities stemming from any given subject development.[35] The original intent was to build a calculator which could automate the determination of impact fees based on any given live 3D geometry of a building or master plan. The base multipliers were based on estimates from the lifelong work of Arthur C. Nelson and were updated for NYC budgets and stated levels of service standards.[36] The variation between Nelson's baseline figures and those calculated for NYC were surprisingly consistent with largest disparity attributable to higher labor and pension costs in NYC.[37]

The one major deviation from Nelson's work relates to the assigned unit cost of storm water infrastructure. The $33 per square foot based on a per capita allocation of 375 square feet represents one of two possible scenarios. First, it is an aggregate cost of a variety of storm water management interventions from pumping to culvert construction which can be widely distributed and utilized in any given zone. Second, the aggregate sums are a proportionate measure of what it would mean to capture some value (i.e., surtax) in the development to pay for the estimated $15 billion needed to protect NYC from rising sea level rise, increased volume of rain in less frequent occurrences and other such negative impacts of climate change. Therefore, the aggregate sums collected for storm water in Scenario #1 are roughly 30% of mitigation costs for a 30% capture of the additional one million New Yorkers and almost 50% for almost 50% of the capture in Scenario #2. There would be some serious concerns relating to equitability for taxing new residents and workers for the benefit of all; however, the numbers represent an interesting evaluation of the

---

35. *See generally*, James C. Nicholas, Arthur C. Nelson & Julian C. Juergensmeyer, A PRACTITIONER'S GUIDE TO DEVELOPMENT IMPACT FEES (American Planning Association 1991).

36. Arthur C. Nelson, *Reforming Infrastructure Financing in a Fiscally Constrained World*, Metropolitan Research Center, University of Utah (2010) at Table 1: Estimate of Costs to Support 100 Million New Americans 2010-2040.

37. One shortcoming of this approach as presented is that marginal transportation costs are not calculated. This is partially attributable to a lack of a defensible multiplier which is specific to NYC's MTA. Unsubsidized ridership estimates are highly skewed due to the large levels of capital expenditures which burden the system and do not provide an accurate reflection of true cost. This is an area of future research which is critical to advancing the comprehensiveness of the technique cited herein.

potential to capture value which allows real estate projects to at least pay for their proportionate share of the infrastructure burden. Accordingly, both scenarios include the development of seawall and dyke construction on all coastal or littoral zones.

The early ambition of the subject project was to create a parametric user interface similar to the FIELD (fiscal impact estimates of land development) platform utilized in Florida, but with the additional ability to communicate and visualize alternative development options and their corresponding project economics.[38] From a public policy point of view, the FIELD platform offered public and private parties alike a consistent level of transparency and predictability in anticipating the impact price of any given development. This application was a direct result of Florida statutes which require an Evaluation and Appraisal Reports of comprehensive plans so that government officials can understand,

> [T]he financial feasibility of implementing the comprehensive plan and of providing needed infrastructure to achieve and maintain adopted level of service standards and sustain concurrency management system through capital improvements element, as well as the ability to address infrastructure backlogs and meet the demands of growth on public services and facilities.[39]

Impact fees are just one mechanism to manage growth and their application has not been without controversy. The quote above highlights a critical debate as to whether the impact fee payor should pay for costs of amenities they directly receive in their development or whether they are paying for capital costs external to their immediate impact, including deferred capital costs. This is the exact highlighted dilemma that faces NYC in the face of sea level rise.

For instance, in Table 3, the evenly rounded estimated costs of public service personnel are based on per capita baseline compensation, plus the corresponding pension contributions which have increased in recent years to maintain normalized funding levels. For police and firefighters, this equals roughly 23% of 2011 gross pay, which is consistent with projected 2012 contribution rates of 21%.[40] Assuming this method

---

38. Hillsborough County Planning Commission, Fiscal Impact Estimates of Land Development (FIELD)(2009)(available at http://www.tpcfieldmodel.org/FIELD)(last accessed October 10, 2012); see generally, Zenia Kotval and John Mullin, Fiscal Impact Analysis: Methods, Cases and Intellectual Debate, Lincoln Land Institute (September 2006).

39. Florida Statutes, Chapter 163.3191(2)(a)-(c).

40. E.J. McMahon and Josh Barro, New York's Exploding Pension Costs, Empire Center for New York State Policy, SR8-11 (2010) at Table 1.

were codified, it raises a number of questions relating to the underlying equitability of landowners, renters and homebuyers bearing the costs of pension funds who might be either poorly managed at worst and simply unlucky like everyone else at best.

The ultimate question is whether and to what extent these parties will directly or indirectly bear the cost of impact fees. This test of proximity is generally mediated by state statue. Although 28 states have enabling legislation for impact fees, New York does not. However, New York state courts have held that impact fees fall within the defined limits of home-rule despite a lack of formal enabling legislation.[41] Despite this expansive view of local home-rule power, NYC has never adopted impact fee legislation. Part of this reluctance stems from developers and local community groups who are reluctant to experiment with impact fees as both parties are unsure whether or not the cost of the impact fees—or some disproportionate percentage thereof—will be absorbed by the landowners or will be directly passed on to consumers. The existing literature which suggests that prices increase somewhat inconsistently in both new (proxy for immediate consumer absorption) and existing housing development (proxy for land price absorption) is largely focused on suburban housing and does not account for the comparative and relative inelastic demand for housing in NYC.[42] As noted by Vicki Bean, the empirical evidence is inconclusive as to whether impact fees have a negative impact on the affordability and supply of housing; and, as such, the window for future research is wide-open.[43]

The approach taken hereof for calculating impacts is intended to give the reader a generalizable understanding of the scale of the

---

41. Barnard V. Keenan, *A Perspective: New York Communities and Impact Fees*, 7 Pace Envt'l. L. Rev. 2, 329 (1990); Arizona: 1988 Ariz. Rev. Stat. Ann., § 9-463.05 (cities), § 11-1102 et seq.; Arkansas: 2003 Arkansas Code, § 14-56-103; California: 1989 Cal. Gov't Code, § 66000 et seq.; Colorado: 2001 Colo. Rev. Stat., § 29-20-104.5; § 29-1-801804; § 22-54-102; Florida: 2006 Fla. Stat., § 163.31801; Georgia: 1990 Ga. Code Ann., § 36-71-1 et seq.; Hawaii: 1992 Haw. Rev. Stat., § 46-141 et seq.; § 264-121 et seq.; § 320; Idaho: 1992 Idaho Code, § 67-8201 et seq.; Illinois: 1987 605 Ill. Comp. Stat. Ann., § 5/5-901 et seq.; Indiana: 1991 Ind. Code Ann., § 36-7-4-1300 et seq.; Maine: 1988 Me. Rev. State. Ann., Title 30-A, § 4354; Maryland: 1992 Maryland Code, Art. 25B, § 13D; Montana: 2005 Montana Code Annotated, Title 7, Chapter 6, Part 16; Nevada: 1989 Nev. Rev. Stat., § 278B; New Hampshire: 1991 N.H. Rev. Stat. Ann., § 674:21; New Jersey: 1989 N.J. Perm. Stat., § 27:1C-1 et seq.; § 40:55D-42; New Mexico: 1993 New Mexico Stat. Ann., § 5-8-1 et seq.; Oregon: 1991 Or. Rev. State, § 223.297 et seq.; Pennsylvania: 1990 Pa. Stat. Ann., Title 53, § 10502-A et seq.; Rhode Island: 2000 General Laws of Rhode Island, §45-22.4; South Carolina: 1999 Code of Laws of S.C. § 6-1-910 et seq.; Texas: 1987 Tex. Local Gov't Code Ann., Title 12, § 395.001 et seq.; Utah: 1995 Utah Code, § 11-36-101 et. seq.; Vermont: 1989 Vt. Stat. Ann., Title 24, § 5200 et seq.; Virginia: 1990 Va. Code Ann., § 15.2-2317 et seq.; Washington: 1991 RCW, § 82.02.050 et seq.; West Virginia: 1990 W. Va. Code, § 7-20-1 et seq.; and Wisconsin: 1993 Wis. Stats. § 66.0617.

infrastructure, both human and physical, which will be need to accommodate the next generation of New Yorkers. However, the applications are not limited to impact fees as there is an emerging sub-field of study known as 'value capture' which could benefit from these aggregate calculations and corresponding managed work-flow.[44] The general impetus behind value capture is the development and testing of planning instruments which capture through fees or taxes some percentage increase in the value of real estate which is spatially proximate to investments made by the public from which said private property owners accrue some additional value or benefit. The recent interest in this field by academics and practitioners is a reflection of the necessity to think out of the box given the difficulties facing the financing and provision of infrastructure in the present fiscally constrained atmosphere.

Historically in the U.S., impact fees, tax increment financing, public-private partnerships and special assessments have been the predominate mechanisms for value capture. However, recent scholarship has examined a variety of jurisdictions from Great Brittan to Brazil which have implemented a number of novel instruments, such as the U.K.'s land value tax, which is a type of betterment tax that levies on the increased value attributable to the land and not the improvements by virtue of the public's investments in infrastructure.[45] In Brazil, governments have resorted to something very similar to the Cap and Trade proposition cited herein whereas properties are set to a baseline FAR (often a product of downzoning) and additional FAR is either directly sold or auctioned on the market.[46]

42. Charles J. Delaney, and Marc T. Smith, *Impact Fees and the Price of New Housing: An Empirical Study, AREUAE Journal 17*: 41–54 (1989); Charles J. Delaney and Marc T. Smith, *Pricing Implications of Development Exactions on Existing Housing Stock, Growth and Change 20*: 1–12 (1989); Larry D. Singell and Jane H. Lillydahl, *Housing Impact Fees*, 66 LAND ECONOMICS 1, 82–92 (1990); Arthur C. Nelson, et al., *Price Effects of Road and Other Impact Fees on Urban Land*, TRANSPORTATION RESEARCH RECORD 1305: 36–41 (1992); Andrejs Skaburskis, and Mohammad Qadeer, *An Empirical Estimation of the Price Effects of Development Impact Fees*, 29 URBAN STUDIES 653–667 (1992); Marla Dresch and Steven M. Sheffrin, *Who Pays for Development Fees and Exactions?* San Francisco: Public Policy Institute of California (1997); Keith Ihlanfeldt and Timothy M. Shaughnessy, *An Empirical Investigation of the Effects of Impact Fees on Housing and Land Markets*, 34 REGIONAL SCIENCE AND URBAN ECONOMICS 639–661 (2004).

43. Vicki Bean, *Impact Fees and Housing Affordability*, 8 CITYSCAPE 1, 139 (2005) at 168.

44. *See*, Gregory K. Ingram and Yu-Hung Ho, eds., VALUE CAPTURE AND LAND POLICIES (Lincoln Institute of Land Policy 2011).

45. Frances Plimmer and Greg McGill, *Land Value Taxation: Betterment Taxation in England and the Potential for Change*, Paper Presented at International Federation of Surveyors (FIG) Working Week (April 2003).

46. Paulo Henrique Sandroni, *Recent Experience with Land Value Capture in São Paulo, Brazil*, Land Lines (Lincoln Institute of Land Policy July 2011).

This upfront expense, which may or may not have the concurrency requirements of an impact fee, highlight the tension inherent in value captures schemes—at what point must one realize or recognize (borrowing from the language of U.S. tax law) the attributable increase in value? Given the timing mechanism for payment, are you better off with a value capture scheme or are you better off paying higher base property taxes over the long-run for the same level of service? One advantage for value capture speaks to this notion of equal levels of services. Mechanisms such as Brazil's urban operations and the U.S.'s tax increment financing do provide for de facto concurrency in that the specific infrastructure expenditures are linked to specific geographies which are the subject of the value capture. In a conventional property tax system, a lack of corresponding linkage is a great source of political acrimony, especially when it comes to capital improvements wherein the perception (and often reality) is that one part of town is unfairly subsidizing the development of another part of town.[47]

Ultimately, the greatest single impediment to the proliferation of value capture schemes is the lack of empirical data which affirmatively as matter of causation and proximity links the creation of value, if only the fiction thereof, to any specific public investment or any specific catchment area. For instance, econometric studies in the U.S. which have attempted to identify value derived from public transportation have found very little impact exceeding a 10% premium within an approximate half-mile influence.[48] With exception to tax increment financing, this lack of empirical evidence stands as a barrier to definitively identifying a district, much less a building, which is the subject of the value capture which is a result of the public's larger infrastructural and place making vision.

---

47. This phenomenon is closely linked to the history of municipal annexation in the U.S. wherein central business districts subsidized suburban expansion at the cost of maintaining urban services and infrastructure.

48. C. Atkinson-Palombo, *Comparing the Capitalization Benefits of Light Rail Transit and Overlay Zoning for Single Family Houses and Condos by Neighborhood Type in Metropolitan Phoenix*, 47 URBAN STUDIES 2409-2426 (2010); M. Duncan, *The Impact of Transit-Oriented Development on Housing Prices in San Diego, CA.*, 48 URBAN STUDIES 101-127 (2011); *see generally*, N. Baum-Snow and M. Kahn, *The Effects of New Public Projects to Expand Urban Rail Transit*, 77 J. OF PUBLIC ECONOMICS 241-263 (2000); R. Cervero and M. Duncan, *Transit's Valued-Added Effects: Light and Commuter Rail Services and Commercial Land Values*, Transportation Research Record, 1805, 8-15 (2002); D.B. Hess and T.M. Almeida, *Impact of Proximity to Light Rail Transit on Station-area Property Values in Buffalo, New York*, 44 URBAN STUDIES 1041-1068 (2007).

URBAN BENCHMARKING

The final point of analysis for the resulting space allocations is a process of urban benchmarking wherein certain physical and environmental metrics are measured against each other by and between zones and the city at-large. The criteria for these metrics are identified in Appendix Table 8. These metrics consider relative access to mass-transit, jobs, retail programs and public space. The implicit humanist perspective of measuring distances and spaces and then assigning a measured proportionality underscores the attempt to underwrite a proxy for the experiential meaning of living and working in these simulated urban conditions. More specific to the scenarios herein, the zones are benchmarked against an agglomerated sample of Manhattan neighbors. This Manhattanization of analysis advances the notion of hyper density being tested in this project. This should not be confused with the cultural imposition of Manhattan as this represents only the physical comparison thereof.

To facilitate this understanding, the measured criteria are qualitatively ranked and ordered in a series of weighted indices relating to density, public space and walkability. A more detailed weighting for each index can be found in Appendix Table 8. The first point of analysis relates to contextual zone population density. Because the urban benchmarking tool is based on the Pluto data set, population is measured as a net function of residential square footage. This data set does not give any insight as to unit vacancy, quality or marketability. However, sample selection data from ESRI was cross-checked with the results from the Pluto calculations and the population numbers generally varied by less than 10%. Inconsistencies can be attributed to overlaps between zone boundaries and the sub-aggregations of the ESRI database (zip codes, census tracts, etc...). For zones which are themselves mega projects, a half (.5) mile influence was measured to give a broader context of the zone to its surroundings districts or neighborhoods.

The same techniques are applied for commercial, retail and industrial classifications to measure job density. These numbers are most likely less reliable than the residential population figures due to the varied level of job activity within these non-residential classifications. While average square feet works well enough for office and retail workers, industrial and manufacturing land uses may not be indicative of the same level of real estate productivity. As a result of measured industrial productivity (vacancies, identified employers, etc..), the corresponding workforce has a much lower per capital level of allocated square footage than do office and retail workers. Due to the relative strength and weakness of the population figures, the density index weights various built environment metrics (65%) much higher than population density (20%) and job density (15%). The internal weighting within the density index is somewhat circular to the extent the population and jobs are measured as a function of the square footage, which would indicate that it is essentially weighted against itself. The counter argument is that there are zones which have a lot of capacity and built space but very little population, and, as such, the index should differentiate between the two (population v. space) for purposes of comparing subtle distinctions of density within an already built up urban area.

The remaining indices relate to walkability and public space. The public space index measures and weights both public and open space within the zone. The index also includes calculations for retail and sky exposure. The former is reflection of the programming trends in urban landscaping, which, if anything, are borne out of the necessity of public spaces to pay for themselves in terms of operations and capital investments. The latter is a proxy for the qualitatively positive experience of traversing the city in the sunshine—otherwise defined as the Street Sky Exposure Score, as noted in Appendix Table 9. This score is a composite measurement in Rhino which utilizes a combination of surface contouring, light projecting and environmental conditioning simulations. The rationale is to evaluate the experiential quality of the space in terms of light and air. In isolation these measurements do not mean much. However, when the scores are aggregated, it is possible to decipher distinctions in the patternization of the density allocated in both of the scenarios. " The results seem to indicate that beyond a certain level of density, additional density under Scenario #2 has very little impact on the metrics as compared with Scenario #1 versus the status quo.

The final index relates to the concept of walkability. Walk scores have become a popular interface for real estate brokerage firms to highlight neighborhood amenities.[49] The least sophisticated of these scores simply measures the distance, inclusive of a distance decay function, from a particular address to a variety of public and private amenities. The observed amenities are then weighted with grocery stores and restaurants getting priority over book stores and entertainment venues, for instance.[50] These distances are then weighted against intersection density and block length. This type of analysis works well in suburban and some urban conditions, but does not provide an accurate reflection of the walkability

49. *See*, walkscore.com (last accessed December 1, 2012).

50. *See*, www2.walkscore.com/pdf/WalkScoreMethodology.pdf (last accessed December 1, 2012).

within the highly urbanized context of NYC.[51] For instance, virtually all of Manhattan would score a perfect score of a 100 at walkscore.com despite the reality that walkability, particularly retail access, can vary greatly within the borough. More sophisticated walk scoring techniques measure and include criminal activity, pedestrian safety, optimal route simulations and proximity to green space.[52]

The walkability index utilized herein takes a slightly different approach. Because of the relative concentration of retail, which is already measured in the public space index, the walkability index specifically excludes retail access in its calculations. Instead, the index focuses on modes of travel (subway, bus, bike, and walking) and estimated trip times (not including mass transit) based on a walking trip through the longest linear traverse of the zone. In this sense, the index is more a measure of accessibility than the conventions of walkability. Given the unique nature of NYC wherein most trips contain a combination of walking and mass transit, the index is an attempt to reframe the interplay between accessibility and walkability in a truly urban context. The final component of the index borrows from the public space methodology in that it attempts to measure the physicality of the urban context as a means of promoting a qualitatively positive walking experience. Therefore, street widths, which are a reliable proxy for sidewalk widths, block sizes, intersection density and street wall continuity are all measured and weighted so as to provide some meaning between the physicalities of the street and the experience and efficacy of urban transit.

The urban benchmarking calculators utilized in this report leave room for plenty of future research in the calibration of the metrics and the associated nuance of behaviors which are difficult to simulate. The application of flow dynamic models at the street and building scale may also prove useful to the extent that program behavior is a reflection of actual behavior. Almost all of the metrics are oriented towards a subjective qualitative determination as to an absolute. For instance, does a continuous street wall always (or, even sometimes) result in a more positive walking experience? The answer is probably not. However, there is a subjective aesthetic norm which argues that continuous street wall at a certain height does provide a sense of urban continuity in the experience which

51. *See generally*, Dustin T. Duncan, et. al, *Validation of Walk Score® for Estimating Neighborhood Walkability: An Analysis for Four US Metropolitan Areas*, 8 Int. J. Environ. Res. Public Health 4160-4179 (2011).

52. *See generally*, Lucas Carr, et. al, *Validation of Walk Score for Estimating Access to Walkable Amenities*, 45 Br. J. Sports Med 1144-1148 (2011); Ko Ko Lwin and Yuji Murayama, *Modeling of Urban Green Space Walkability: Eco-friendly Walk Score Calculator*, 35 Computers, Environment And Urban Systems 408-420 (2011).

is recognized by the planning and design professions as being uniformly positive.[53]

The subjective nature of the benchmarking underscores its universal application across all neighborhoods and the cultures to which they engender. However, it does serve the purpose of providing a baseline from which to compare the positive and negative impacts of the density allocations which are the subject of this report. To many, density is conceptualized narrowly in terms of its negative implications. As such, the benchmarking exercise is an attempt to communicate the nuances which in the aggregate make up the daily lives of urban residents. It is only through the process of disentangling the notion of experience, whether grounded physically or psychologically, that we can attempt to flesh out the negatives and positives of increased urban density.

---

53. *See generally*, Allen B. Jacobs, GREAT STREETS (MIT Press 2001); Allen B. Jacobs, Elizabeth MacDonald and Yodan Rofe, THE BOULEVARD BOOK: HISTORY, EVOLUTION, DESIGN OF MULTIWAY BOULEVARDS (MIT Press 2003); Kenneth Frampton, *The Generic Street as a Continuous Built Form*, in ON STREETS (MIT Press 1986).

III. NEW YORK CITY

WILLET'S POINT

SHERIDAN EXPRESSWAY

QUEENS BOULEVARD

SOUTH CONCOURSE

125TH STREET

LONG ISLAND CITY

WEST SIDE

SEWARD PARK

DOWNTOWN MANHATTAN

RED HOOK

ST. GEORGE / STAPLETON

BROOKLYN WATERFRONT

DOWNTOWN BROOKLYN

ATLANTIC YARDS

ATLANTIC AVENUE

0.5 1   2 mi

NEW YORK CITY TOTAL ZONES
SIMULATION RESULTS

	SCENARIO 01			SCENARIO 02		
DEVELOPMENT METRICS						
	($) 2012	(FV) 2040 @ 3%	(PV) 2040 @ 10%	($) 2012	(FV) 2040 @ 3%	(PV) 2040 @ 10%
Total Development Cost*	$97.68	$149.76	$32.46	$155.41	$238.28	$51.65
Total Equity*	$29.30	$44.92	$9.73	$46.56	$71.38	$15.47
Total Market Value*	$151.28	$213.94	$50.28	$231.21	$354.50	$76.84
Total FAR of New Development	177,683,609			286,699,424		
Total Square Feet (Sq. Ft.)	139,683,419			237,140,392		
Total Residential Sq. Ft.	31,324,271			38,757,192		
Total Office Sq. Ft.	6,653,773			11,431,840		
Total Retail Sq. Ft.	107,364			181,486		
Total Residential Units	9,081			10,717		
IMPACT METRICS						
Total Annual Impact	$1,137,357,759			$2,793,474,394		
Total Annual Impact Per Capita	$4,087.48			$5,913.48		
Total Nonrecurring Impact	$4,108,825,669			$9,073,458,222		
Total Nonrecurring Impact Per Capita	$14,766.47			$19,207.51		
Total Stormwater	$3,909,608,401			$8,488,105,069		
POPULATION & JOB METRICS						
Resident Population	278,254			472,391		
Construction Jobs	1,011,284			1,881,326		
Office Jobs	235,521			291,407		
Retail Jobs	133,075			228,637		
CITY & STATE ANNUAL TAX REVENUE, ($) 2012						
Property	$2,448	Million		$8,396	Million	
Sales	$953	Million		$2,364	Million	
Employment	$334	Million		$2,015	Million	
TOTAL	$3,735	Million		$12,775	Million	

* Billions

IV. MANHATTAN

125TH STREET

WEST SIDE

SEWARD PARK

LOWER MANHATTAN

0.5   1   2 mi

MANHATTAN AVAILABLE FAR [SQ. FT.]

Total Avail GFA	635,619,551
Total Avail Resi	175,690,117
Total Avail Comm	88,495,084
Total Avail Mixed	72,502,833
Total Avail Vacant	66,043,776

> 7.10
5.10 - 7.00
3.10 - 5.00
1.10 - 3.00
0.00 - 1.00

CURE. NYC 2040

MANHATTAN DEVELOPMENT INDEX*

Total Avail GFA	125,793,642
Total Avail Resi	10,643,830
Total Avail Comm	28,166,746
Total Avail Mixed	3,602,264
Total Avail Vacant	52,914,624

■ 0.60 - 1.00
□ 0.30 - 0.59
■ 0.00 - 0.29

*Areas taken from lots with scores of 0.60 or higher.

WEST SIDE
SIMULATION RESULTS

	SCENARIO 01			SCENARIO 02		
	DEVELOPMENT METRICS					
	($) 2012	(FV) 2040 @ 3%	(PV) 2040 @ 10%	($) 2012	(FV) 2040 @ 3%	(PV) 2040 @ 10%
Total Development Cost				$34.71	$53.21 Billion	$11.53 Billion
Total Equity				$10.41	$15.96 Billion	$3.46 Billion
Total Market Value				$69.43	$106.45 Billion	$23.07 Billion
Total FAR of New Development				17.68		
Total Square Feet (Sq. Ft.)	42,500,000	*Simulation Not Applicable; Based on Actual Megaproject.		57,851,563		
Total Residential Sq. Ft.	17,500,000			29,500,090		
Total Office Sq. Ft.	13,451			27,000,000		
Total Retail Sq. Ft.	24,000,000			1,351,473		
Total Residential Units	13,451			22,675		
Cost	$25.50 Billion					
Value	$53.22 Billion					

	IMPACT METRICS					
Facility	Service Estimate		Add't Service Cost	Service Estimate		Add't Service Cost
Parks and Recreation				722	Acres	$75,810,551 Annual
Police				1,207	Officers	$133,998,398 Annual
Fire/Emergency Medical				549	Officers	$49,385,159 Annual
Water				28,880,210	Gallons	$52,706,383 Annual
Sewer				21,660,157	Gallons	$79,059,574 Annual
Schools	*Simulation Not Applicable; Based on Actual Megaproject.			8,163	Students	$179,585,483 Annual
Total Annual Impact						$570,545,547
Total Annual Impact Per Capita						$9,709
Stormwater				20,273,966	Sq.Ft.	$669,040,886 Nonrecurring
Public Buildings				144,401	Sq.Ft.	$43,320,315 Nonrecurring
Courts and Justice				144,401	Sq.Ft.	$72,200,525 Nonrecurring
Libraries				144,401	Sq.Ft.	$57,760,420 Nonrecurring
Total Nonrecurring Impact						$842,322,145
Total Nonrecurring Impact Per Capita						$14,334

	POPULATION & JOB METRICS	
Resident Population		58,765
Additional Temporary Population		230,037
Construction Jobs	*Simulation Not Applicable; Based on Actual Megaproject.	598,185
Office Jobs		203,008
Retail Jobs		3,003

	CITY & STATE ANNUAL TAX REVENUE, ($) 2012	
Property		$4,110 Million
Sales	*Simulation Not Applicable; Based on Actual Megaproject.	$314 Million
Employment		$1,380 Million
TOTAL		$5,850 Million

WEST SIDE
SCENARIO 01

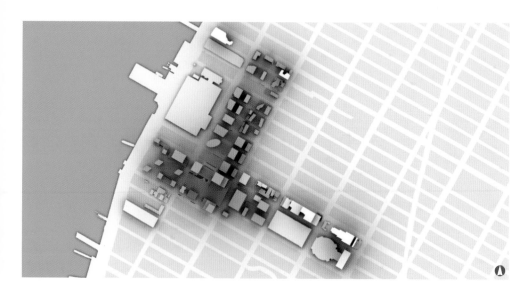

WEST SIDE
SCENARIO 02

Office
Retail
Residential

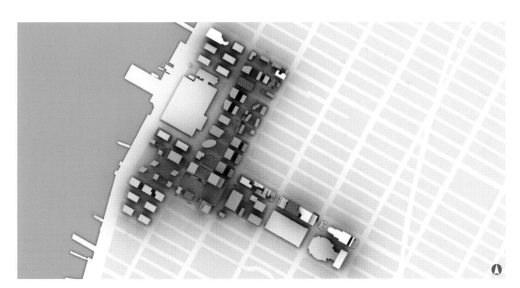

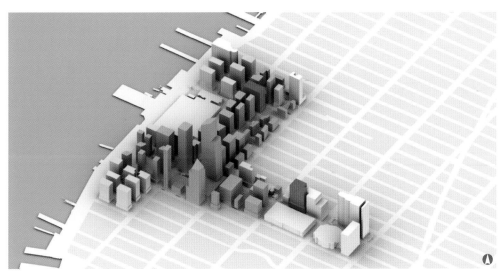

SCENARIO 01   SCENARIO 02

WALK SCORE

5	4	3	2	1
0-2 min	2-5 min	5-8 min	8-10 min	12-15 min

SKY EXPOSURE

0% 100%

 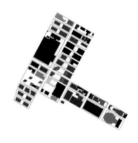

BUILDING HEIGHTS

0	125'	250'	375'	500'

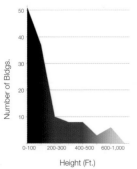 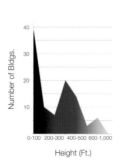

WEST SIDE
URBAN BENCHMARKING

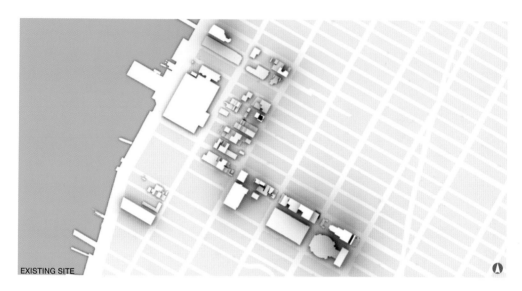

EXISTING SITE

AVERAGE OF MANHATTAN SAMPLE CATCHMENT AREAS	EXISTING	SCENARIO 01	SCENARIO 02
Density	944.5 / 4499.8	1234.4 / 4144.5	4188.5 / 4144.5
Walk Score	4499.8	4144.5	4144.5
Public Space	902.9	1190.1	4097.6
Population Density	1.9 ppl / 5,000 Sq. Ft.	7 ppl / 5,000 Sq. Ft.	14 ppl / 5,000 Sq. Ft.
Job Density	17 jobs / 5,000 Sq. Ft.	28 jobs / 5,000 Sq. Ft.	56 jobs / 5,000 Sq. Ft.
Average FAR	4	15	17.7
Walk Time To Subway	12.2 min	12.2 min	12.2 min
Subway Stops / 0.5 Miles	2.7 stops / 0.5 Mile	2.7 stops / 0.5 Mile	2.7 stops / 0.5 Mile
Bus Stops / 0.5 Miles	10.2 stops / 0.5 Mile	10.2 stops / 0.5 Mile	10.2 stops / 0.5 Mile
Bike Lanes / 5,000 Ft.	5 Ft.	5 Ft.	5 Ft.
Avg Sky Exposure (Parks)	99.7%	80%	80%
Avg Sky Exposure (Streets)	83%	69.5%	64%
Avg Street Width	40 Ft.	40 Ft.	40 Ft.
Avg Intersection Distance	388 Ft.	388 Ft.	388 Ft.
Intersections / 0.5 Miles	177	177	177
Avg Block Perimeter	2194 Ft.	2194 Ft.	2194 Ft.
Avg Street Wall %	0.1%	0.9%	0.9%
Coverage Ratio	50.6%	61.3%	56.3%
Open Space %	30%	23.4%	26.4%
Public Space %	5%	5.8%	5.8%
Retail %	2%	41%	51%

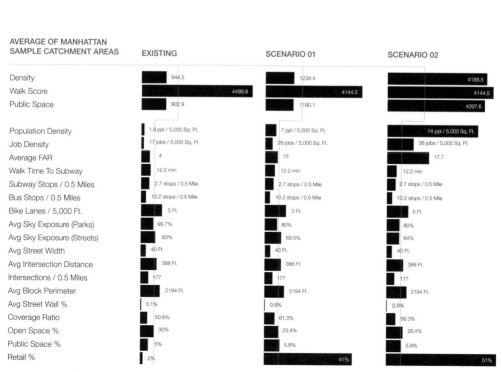

LOWER MANHATTAN
SIMULATION RESULTS

	SCENARIO 01			SCENARIO 02		
DEVELOPMENT METRICS						
	($) 2012	(FV) 2040 @ 3%	(PV) 2040 @ 10%	($) 2012	(FV) 2040 @ 3%	(PV) 2040 @ 10%
Total Development Cost	$8.26	$12.66 Billion	$2.74 Billion	$9.54	$14.62 Billion	$3.17 Billion
Total Equity	$2.47	$3.78 Billion	$0.82 Billion	$2.86	$4.38 Billion	$0.95 Billion
Total Market Value	$14.92	$22.87 Billion	$4.95 Billion	$16.87	$25.86 Billion	$5.60 Billion
Total FAR of New Development	21.47			24.79		
Total Square Feet (Sq. Ft.)	13,772,343			15,900,241		
Total Residential Sq. Ft.	11,814,327			13,942,225		
Total Office Sq. Ft.	776,324			776,324		
Total Retail Sq. Ft.	1,181,692			1,811,692		
Total Residential Units	9,081			10,717		

	IMPACT METRICS					
Facility	Service Estimate		Add't Service Cost	Service Estimate		Add't Service Cost
Parks and Recreation	119	Acres	$12,523,664	Annual	134	Acres	$14,096,025	Annual
Police	199	Officers	$22,136,113	Annual	224	Officers	$24,915,328	Annual
Fire/Emergency Medical	91	Officers	$8,158,272	Annual	102	Officers	$9,182,553	Annual
Water	4,770,920	Gallons	$8,706,928	Annual	5,369,914	Gallons	$9,800,094	Annual
Sewer	3,578,190	Gallons	$13,060,392	Annual	4,027,436	Gallons	$14,700,140	Annual
Schools	3,269	Students	$71,921,191	Annual	3,858	Students	$84,875,036	Annual
Total Annual Impact			$136,506,561				$157,569,177	
Total Annual Impact Per Capita			$5,800				$5,673	
Stormwater	16,459,673	Sq.Ft.	$543,169,193	Nonrecurring	18,526,204	Sq.Ft.	$611,364,745	Nonrecurring
Public Buildings	23,855	Sq.Ft.	$7,156,379	Nonrecurring	26,850	Sq.Ft.	$8,054,871	Nonrecurring
Courts and Justice	23,855	Sq.Ft.	$11,927,299	Nonrecurring	26,850	Sq.Ft.	$13,424,786	Nonrecurring
Libraries	23,855	Sq.Ft.	$9,541,839	Nonrecurring	26,850	Sq.Ft.	$10,739,829	Nonrecurring
Total Nonrecurring Impact			$571,794,711				$643,584,230	
Total Nonrecurring Impact Per Capita			$24,296				$23,172.72	

	POPULATION & JOB METRICS	
Resident Population	23,535	27,773
Additional Temporary Population	24,175	25,926
Construction Jobs	76,922	88,840
Office Jobs	4,086	5,837
Retail Jobs	2,232	2,323

	CITY & STATE ANNUAL TAX REVENUE, ($) 2012			
Property	$421	Million	$468	Million
Sales	$203	Million	$211	Million
Employment	$32	Million	$44	Million
TOTAL	$656	Million	$723	Million

LOWER MANHATTAN

SCENARIO 01

LOWER MANHATTAN
SCENARIO 02

Office
Retail
Residential

SCENARIO 01

SCENARIO 02

WALK SCORE

5   4   3   2   1

0-2 min   2-5 min   5-8 min   8-10 min   12-15 min

SKY EXPOSURE

0%   100%

BUILDING HEIGHTS

0   125'   250'   375'   500'

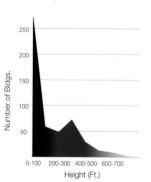
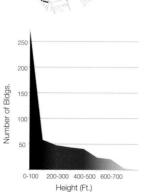

CURE. NYC 2040

LOWER MANHATTAN
URBAN BENCHMARKING

EXISTING SITE

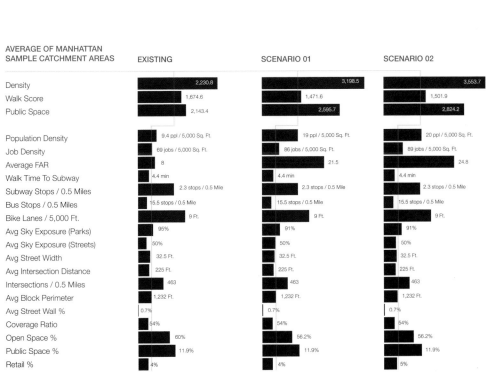

AVERAGE OF MANHATTAN SAMPLE CATCHMENT AREAS	EXISTING	SCENARIO 01	SCENARIO 02
Density	2,230.8	3,198.5	3,553.7
Walk Score	1,674.6	1,471.6	1,501.9
Public Space	2,143.4	2,595.7	2,824.2
Population Density	9.4 ppl / 5,000 Sq. Ft.	19 ppl / 5,000 Sq. Ft.	20 ppl / 5,000 Sq. Ft.
Job Density	69 jobs / 5,000 Sq. Ft.	86 jobs / 5,000 Sq. Ft.	89 jobs / 5,000 Sq. Ft.
Average FAR	8	21.5	24.8
Walk Time To Subway	4.4 min	4.4 min	4.4 min
Subway Stops / 0.5 Miles	2.3 stops / 0.5 Mile	2.3 stops / 0.5 Mile	2.3 stops / 0.5 Mile
Bus Stops / 0.5 Miles	15.5 stops / 0.5 Mile	15.5 stops / 0.5 Mile	15.5 stops / 0.5 Mile
Bike Lanes / 5,000 Ft.	9 Ft.	9 Ft.	9 Ft.
Avg Sky Exposure (Parks)	95%	91%	91%
Avg Sky Exposure (Streets)	50%	50%	50%
Avg Street Width	32.5 Ft.	32.5 Ft.	32.5 Ft.
Avg Intersection Distance	225 Ft.	225 Ft.	225 Ft.
Intersections / 0.5 Miles	463	463	463
Avg Block Perimeter	1,232 Ft.	1,232 Ft.	1,232 Ft.
Avg Street Wall %	0.7%	0.7%	0.7%
Coverage Ratio	54%	54%	54%
Open Space %	60%	56.2%	56.2%
Public Space %	11.9%	11.9%	11.9%
Retail %	4%	4%	5%

125TH STREET
SIMULATION RESULTS

	SCENARIO 01			SCENARIO 02		
	DEVELOPMENT METRICS					
	($) 2012	(FV) 2040 @ 3%	(PV) 2040 @ 10%	($) 2012	(FV) 2040 @ 3%	(PV) 2040 @ 10%
Total Development Cost	$3.16	$4.84 Billion	$1.05 Billion	$6.01	$9.24 Billion	$1.99 Billion
Total Equity	$0.95	$1.45 Billion	$0.31 Billion	$1.80	$2.75 Billion	$0.59 Billion
Total Market Value	$5.72	$8.77 Billion	$1.90 Billion	$10.93	$16.75 Billion	$3.63 Billion
Total FAR of New Development	17.97			13.07		
Total Square Feet (Sq. Ft.)	5,274,867			10,025,082		
Total Residential Sq. Ft.	4,520,823			8,520,107		
Total Office Sq. Ft.	297,224			622,275		
Total Retail Sq. Ft.	456,820			882,700		
Total Residential Units	3,475			6,549		

	IMPACT METRICS					
Facility	Service Estimate		Add't Service Cost		Service Estimate		Add't Service Cost
Parks and Recreation	51	Acres	$5,348,907	Annual	97	Acres	$10,133,358	Annual
Police	85	Officers	$9,454,423	Annual	161	Officers	$17,911,145	Annual
Fire/Emergency Medical	39	Officers	$3,484,431	Annual	73	Officers	$6,601,159	Annual
Water	2,037,679	Gallons	$3,718,764	Annual	3,860,327	Gallons	$7,045,097	Annual
Sewer	1,528,259	Gallons	$5,578,146	Annual	2,895,245	Gallons	$10,567,645	Annual
Schools	1,251	Students	$27,521,075	Annual	2,454	Students	$53,983,398	Annual
Total Annual Impact			$56,228,607				$106,241,803	
Total Annual Impact Per Capita			$6,119				$6,260	
Stormwater	7,029,993	Sq.Ft.	$231,989,759	Nonrecurring	13,318,128	Sq.Ft.	$439,498,231	Nonrecurring
Public Buildings	4,503	Sq.Ft.	$1,350,844	Nonrecurring	19,302	Sq.Ft.	$5,790,491	Nonrecurring
Courts and Justice	4,503	Sq.Ft.	$2,251,406	Nonrecurring	19,302	Sq.Ft.	$9,650,818	Nonrecurring
Libraries	4,503	Sq.Ft.	$1,801,125	Nonrecurring	19,302	Sq.Ft.	$7,720,654	Nonrecurring
Total Nonrecurring Impact			$237,393,133				$462,660,193	
Total Nonrecurring Impact Per Capita			$26,361				$27,260	

	POPULATION & JOB METRICS	
Resident Population	9,006	16,972
Additional Temporary Population	11,371	21,631
Construction Jobs	29,463	56,043
Office Jobs	2,235	3,977
Retail Jobs	1,015	1,962

	CITY & STATE ANNUAL TAX REVENUE, ($) 2012			
Property	$161	Million	$310	Million
Sales	$78	Million	$150	Million
Employment	$17	Million	$31	Million
TOTAL	$256	Million	$491	Million

125TH STREET

SCENARIO 01

125TH STREET

SCENARIO 02

Office
Retail
Residential

SCENARIO 01

SCENARIO 02

WALK SCORE

5	4	3	2	1
0-2 min	2-5 min	5-8 min	8-10 min	12-15 min

SKY EXPOSURE

0%   100%

BUILDING HEIGHTS

0   125'   250'   375'   500'

CURE. NYC 2040

125TH STREET

URBAN BENCHMARKING

EXISTING SITE

AVERAGE OF MANHATTAN SAMPLE CATCHMENT AREAS	EXISTING	SCENARIO 01	SCENARIO 02
Density	721.8	2,441.9	1,915.3
Walk Score	789.0	1,559.0	1,558.1
Public Space	748.2	1,937.7	1,584.5
Population Density	0.7 ppl / 5,000 Sq. Ft.	11 ppl / 5,000 Sq. Ft.	20 ppl / 5,000 Sq. Ft.
Job Density	3 jobs / 5,000 Sq. Ft.	9 jobs / 5,000 Sq. Ft.	15 jobs / 5,000 Sq. Ft.
Average FAR	18	18	25
Walk Time To Subway	7.5 min	7.5 min	7.5 min
Subway Stops / 0.5 Miles	5.6 stops / 0.5 Mile	5.6 stops / 0.5 Mile	5.6 stops / 0.5 Mile
Bus Stops / 0.5 Miles	33.4 stops / 0.5 Mile	33.4 stops / 0.5 Mile	33.4 stops / 0.5 Mile
Bike Lanes / 5,000 Ft.	17 Ft.	17 Ft.	17 Ft.
Avg Sky Exposure (Parks)	99.5%	95%	95%
Avg Sky Exposure (Streets)	89%	87.5%	87.5%
Avg Street Width	65 Ft.	65 Ft.	65 Ft.
Avg Intersection Distance	360 Ft.	360 Ft.	360 Ft.
Intersections / 0.5 Miles	127	127	127
Avg Block Perimeter	1,404 Ft.	1,404 Ft.	1,404 Ft.
Avg Street Wall %	0.6%	0.6%	0.6%
Coverage Ratio	68.4%	61.4%	61.4%
Open Space %	16.8%	23.4%	23.4%
Public Space %	16.8%	16.8%	16.8%
Retail %	25%	51%	51%

SEWARD PARK

SIMULATION RESULTS

	SCENARIO 01			SCENARIO 02		
DEVELOPMENT METRICS						
	($) 2012	(FV) 2040 @ 3%	(PV) 2040 @ 10%	($) 2012	(FV) 2040 @ 3%	(PV) 2040 @ 10%
Total Development Cost	$4.26	$6.53 Billion	$1.41 Billion	$5.88	$9.01 Billion	$1.95 Billion
Total Equity	$1.28	$1.96 Billion	$0.42 Billion	$1.76	$2.69 Billion	$0.58 Billion
Total Market Value	$7.70	$11.91 Billion	$2.58 Billion	$10.24	$15.70 Billion	$3.40 Billion
Total FAR of New Development	14.03			16.17		
Total Square Feet (Sq. Ft.)	7,116,650			9,813,662		
Total Residential Sq. Ft.	6,112,333			8,533,744		
Total Office Sq. Ft.	401,718			575,580		
Total Retail Sq. Ft.	602,599			704,338		
Total Residential Units	4,696			6,559		

IMPACT METRICS							
Facility	Service Estimate		Add't Service Cost		Service Estimate		Add't Service Cost	
Parks and Recreation	68	Acres	$7,152,699	Annual	89	Acres	$9,296,154	Annual
Police	114	Officers	$12,642,703	Annual	148	Officers	$16,431,350	Annual
Fire/Emergency Medical	52	Officers	$4,659,473	Annual	67	Officers	$6,055,780	Annual
Water	2,724,838	Gallons	$4,972,829	Annual	3,541,392	Gallons	$6,463,040	Annual
Sewer	2,043,628	Gallons	$7,459,244	Annual	2,656,044	Gallons	$9,694,560	Annual
Schools	1,691	Students	$37,209,591	Annual	2,361	Students	$51,950,232	Annual
Total Annual Impact			$74,096,538				$99,891,117	
Total Annual Impact Per Capita			$6,085				$5,876	
Stormwater	9,400,690	Sq.Ft.	$310,222,786	Nonrecurring	12,217,802	Sq.Ft.	$403,187,470	Nonrecurring
Public Buildings	13,624	Sq.Ft.	$4,087,257	Nonrecurring	17,707	Sq.Ft.	$5,312,088	Nonrecurring
Courts and Justice	13,624	Sq.Ft.	$6,812,095	Nonrecurring	17,707	Sq.Ft.	$8,853,480	Nonrecurring
Libraries	13,624	Sq.Ft.	$5,449,676	Nonrecurring	17,707	Sq.Ft.	$7,082,784	Nonrecurring
Total Nonrecurring Impact			$326,571,813				$424,435,822	
Total Nonrecurring Impact Per Capita			$26,821				$24,968	

POPULATION & JOB METRICS		
Resident Population	12,176	16,999
Additional Temporary Population	15,072	18,414
Construction Jobs	39,724	54,878
Office Jobs	3,020	4,328
Retail Jobs	1,339	1,565

CITY & STATE ANNUAL TAX REVENUE, ($) 2012				
Property	$217	Million	$290	Million
Sales	$104	Million	$127	Million
Employment	$23	Million	$32	Million
TOTAL	$344	Million	$449	Million

SEWARD PARK

SCENARIO 01

SEWARD PARK

SCENARIO 02

■ Office
■ Retail
■ Residential

SCENARIO 01

SCENARIO 02

WALK SCORE

5	4	3	2	1
0-2 min	2-5 min	5-8 min	8-10 min	12-15 min

SKY EXPOSURE

0%   100%

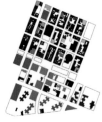

BUILDING HEIGHTS

0	125'	250'	375'	500'

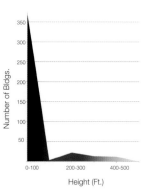

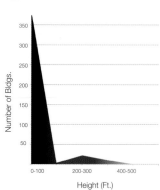

CURE. NYC 2040

SEWARD PARK

URBAN BENCHMARKING

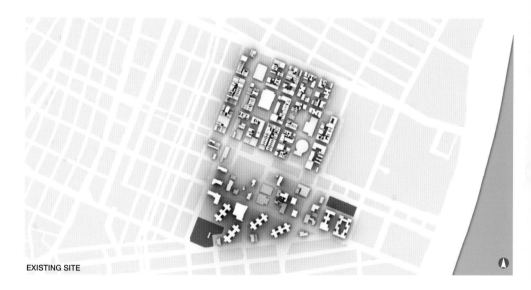

EXISTING SITE

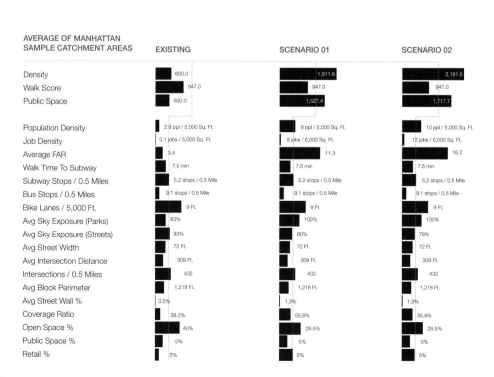

AVERAGE OF MANHATTAN SAMPLE CATCHMENT AREAS	EXISTING	SCENARIO 01	SCENARIO 02
Density	600.0	1,911.8	2,181.5
Walk Score	947.0	947.0	947.0
Public Space	500.0	1,527.4	1,717.7
Population Density	2.9 ppl / 5,000 Sq. Ft.	8 ppl / 5,000 Sq. Ft.	10 ppl / 5,000 Sq. Ft.
Job Density	0.1 jobs / 5,000 Sq. Ft.	9 jobs / 5,000 Sq. Ft.	12 jobs / 5,000 Sq. Ft.
Average FAR	3.4	11.3	16.2
Walk Time To Subway	7.5 min	7.5 min	7.5 min
Subway Stops / 0.5 Miles	5.2 stops / 0.5 Mile	5.2 stops / 0.5 Mile	5.2 stops / 0.5 Mile
Bus Stops / 0.5 Miles	9.1 stops / 0.5 Mile	9.1 stops / 0.5 Mile	9.1 stops / 0.5 Mile
Bike Lanes / 5,000 Ft.	9 Ft.	9 Ft.	9 Ft.
Avg Sky Exposure (Parks)	83%	100%	100%
Avg Sky Exposure (Streets)	83%	80%	78%
Avg Street Width	72 Ft.	72 Ft.	72 Ft.
Avg Intersection Distance	309 Ft.	309 Ft.	309 Ft.
Intersections / 0.5 Miles	432	432	432
Avg Block Perimeter	1,218 Ft.	1,218 Ft.	1,218 Ft.
Avg Street Wall %	0.5%	1.3%	1.3%
Coverage Ratio	38.2%	55.8%	55.8%
Open Space %	40%	28.5%	28.5%
Public Space %	5%	5%	5%
Retail %	3%	5%	5%

V. QUEENS

LONG ISLAND CITY

QUEENS BOULEVARD

WILLET'S POINT

QUEENS AVAILABLE FAR [SQ. FT.]

Total Avail GFA	1,033,602,087
Total Avail Resi	267,515,066
Total Avail Comm	78,006,647
Total Avail Mixed	17,590,295
Total Avail Vacant	95,218,323

> 7.10
5.10 - 7.00
3.10 - 5.00
1.10 - 3.00
0.00 - 1.00

CURE. NYC 2040

QUEENS DEVELOPMENT INDEX*

Total Avail GFA	176,306,719
Total Avail Resi	5,569,431
Total Avail Comm	22,278,685
Total Avail Mixed	217,315
Total Avail Vacant	56,680,775

- 0.60 - 1.00
- 0.30 - 0.59
- 0.00 - 0.29

*Areas taken from lots with scores of 0.60 or higher.

LONG ISLAND CITY
SIMULATION RESULTS

	SCENARIO 01			SCENARIO 02		
DEVELOPMENT METRICS						
	($) 2012	(FV) 2040 @ 3%	(PV) 2040 @ 10%	($) 2012	(FV) 2040 @ 3%	(PV) 2040 @ 10%
Total Development Cost	$8.73	$13.38 Billion	$2.90 Billion	$17.45	$26.76 Billion	$5.79 Billion
Total Equity	$2.62	$4.01 Billion	$0.87 Billion	$5.23	$8.01 Billion	$1.73 Billion
Total Market Value	$10.00	$15.33 Billion	$3.32 Billion	$20.21	$30.98 Billion	$6.71 Billion
Total FAR of New Development	11.77			14.39		
Total Square Feet (Sq. Ft.)	14,564,194			29,093,559		
Total Residential Sq. Ft.	13,208,841			25,021,711		
Total Office Sq. Ft.	1,041,737			3,293,298		
Total Retail Sq. Ft.	313,616			778,550		
Total Residential Units	10,153			19,233		

IMPACT METRICS						
Facility	Service Estimate		Add't Service Cost		Service Estimate		Add't Service Cost	
Parks and Recreation	101	Acres	$10,609,557	Annual	225	Acres	$23,671,380	Annual
Police	169	Officers	$18,752,847	Annual	377	Officers	$41,840,178	Annual
Fire/Emergency Medical	77	Officers	$6,911,369	Annual	171	Officers	$15,420,213	Annual
Water	4,041,736	Gallons	$7,376,168	Annual	9,017,668	Gallons	$16,457,245	Annual
Sewer	3,031,302	Gallons	$11,064,253	Annual	6,763,251	Gallons	$24,685,867	Annual
Schools	3,655	Students	$80,410,469	Annual	6,924	Students	$152,322,791	Annual
Total Annual Impact			$135,124,664				$274,397,675	
Total Annual Impact Per Capita			$5,135				$5,505	
Stormwater	13,943,990	Sq.Ft.	$460,151,658	Nonrecurring	31,110,956	Sq.Ft.	$1,026,661,558	Nonrecurring
Public Buildings	20,209	Sq.Ft.	$6,062,604	Nonrecurring	45,088	Sq.Ft.	$13,526,503	Nonrecurring
Courts and Justice	20,209	Sq.Ft.	$10,104,340	Nonrecurring	45,088	Sq.Ft.	$22,544,171	Nonrecurring
Libraries	20,209	Sq.Ft.	$8,083,472	Nonrecurring	45,088	Sq.Ft.	$18,035,337	Nonrecurring
Total Nonrecurring Impact			$484,402,075				$1,080,767,569	
Total Nonrecurring Impact Per Capita			$18,410				$21,683	

POPULATION & JOB METRICS		
Resident Population	26,312	49,844
Additional Temporary Population	14,105	40,333
Construction Jobs	82,172	165,401
Office Jobs	7,833	24,762
Retail Jobs	697	1,730

CITY & STATE ANNUAL TAX REVENUE, ($) 2012				
Property	$260	Million	$541	Million
Sales	$92	Million	$201	Million
Employment	$54	Million	$172	Million
TOTAL	$406	Million	$914	Million

LONG ISLAND CITY

SCENARIO 01

LONG ISLAND CITY

SCENARIO 02

- Office
- Retail
- Residential

SCENARIO 01   SCENARIO 02

WALK SCORE

5	4	3	2	1
0-2 min	2-5 min	5-8 min	8-10 min	12-15 min

SKY EXPOSURE

0% ──────────────── 100%

BUILDING HEIGHTS

0	125'	250'	375'	500'

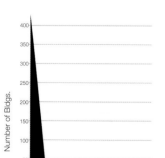 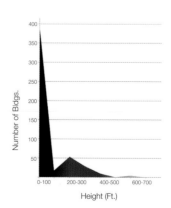

CURE. NYC 2040

LONG ISLAND CITY

URBAN BENCHMARKING

EXISTING SITE

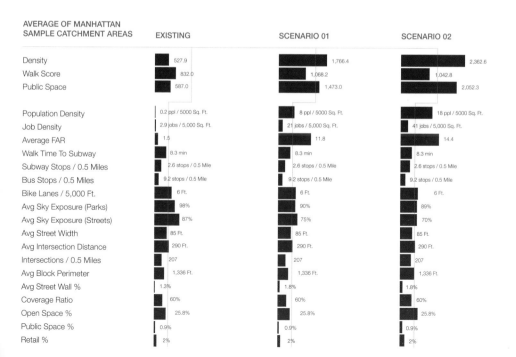

AVERAGE OF MANHATTAN
SAMPLE CATCHMENT AREAS

	EXISTING	SCENARIO 01	SCENARIO 02
Density	527.9	1,766.4	2,362.6
Walk Score	832.0	1,068.2	1,042.8
Public Space	587.0	1,473.0	2,052.3
Population Density	0.2 ppl / 5000 Sq. Ft.	8 ppl / 5000 Sq. Ft.	18 ppl / 5000 Sq. Ft.
Job Density	2.9 jobs / 5,000 Sq. Ft.	21 jobs / 5,000 Sq. Ft.	41 jobs / 5,000 Sq. Ft.
Average FAR	1.5	11.8	14.4
Walk Time To Subway	8.3 min	8.3 min	8.3 min
Subway Stops / 0.5 Miles	2.6 stops / 0.5 Mile	2.6 stops / 0.5 Mile	2.6 stops / 0.5 Mile
Bus Stops / 0.5 Miles	9.2 stops / 0.5 Mile	9.2 stops / 0.5 Mile	9.2 stops / 0.5 Mile
Bike Lanes / 5,000 Ft.	6 Ft.	6 Ft.	6 Ft.
Avg Sky Exposure (Parks)	98%	90%	89%
Avg Sky Exposure (Streets)	87%	75%	70%
Avg Street Width	85 Ft.	85 Ft.	85 Ft.
Avg Intersection Distance	290 Ft.	290 Ft.	290 Ft.
Intersections / 0.5 Miles	207	207	207
Avg Block Perimeter	1,336 Ft.	1,336 Ft.	1,336 Ft.
Avg Street Wall %	1.3%	1.8%	1.8%
Coverage Ratio	60%	60%	60%
Open Space %	25.8%	25.8%	25.8%
Public Space %	0.9%	0.9%	0.9%
Retail %	2%	2%	2%

QUEENS BOULEVARD

SIMULATION RESULTS

	SCENARIO 01			SCENARIO 02		
DEVELOPMENT METRICS						
	($) 2012	(FV) 2040 @ 3%	(PV) 2040 @ 10%	($) 2012	(FV) 2040 @ 3%	(PV) 2040 @ 10%
Total Development Cost	$7.15	$10.92 Billion	$2.37 Billion	$11.06	$16.95 Billion	$3.67 Billion
Total Equity	$2.14	$3.28 Billion	$0.71 Billion	$3.31	$5.07 Billion	$1.10 Billion
Total Market Value	$9.80	$15.02 Billion	$3.25 Billion	$15.24	$23.36 Billion	$5.06 Billion
Total FAR of New Development	6.48			7.81		
Total Square Feet (Sq. Ft.)	14,313,826			22,133,106		
Total Residential Sq. Ft.	13,039,548			19,833,452		
Total Office Sq. Ft.	1,028,355			1,799,994		
Total Retail Sq. Ft.	245,925			499,660		
Total Residential Units	10,023			15,222		

	IMPACT METRICS							
Facility	Service Estimate		Add't Service Cost		Service Estimate		Add't Service Cost	
Parks and Recreation	97	Acres	$10,139,243	Annual	158	Acres	$16,546,913	Annual
Police	161	Officers	$17,921,547	Annual	263	Officers	$29,247,377	Annual
Fire/Emergency Medical	73	Officers	$6,604,993	Annual	120	Officers	$10,779,132	Annual
Water	3,862,569	Gallons	$7,049,188	Annual	6,303,586	Gallons	$11,504,044	Annual
Sewer	2,896,927	Gallons	$10,573,782	Annual	4,727,689	Gallons	$17,256,066	Annual
Schools	3,608	Students	$79,379,877	Annual	5,480	Students	$120,559,909	Annual
Total Annual Impact			$131,668,629				$205,893,441	
Total Annual Impact Per Capita			$5,069				$5,211	
Stormwater	13,325,862	Sq.Ft.	$439,753,454	Nonrecurring	21,747,371	Sq.Ft.	$717,663,243	Nonrecurring
Public Buildings	19,313	Sq.Ft.	$5,793,853	Nonrecurring	31,518	Sq.Ft.	$9,455,379	Nonrecurring
Courts and Justice	19,313	Sq.Ft.	$9,656,422	Nonrecurring	31,518	Sq.Ft.	$15,758,964	Nonrecurring
Libraries	19,313	Sq.Ft.	$7,725,138	Nonrecurring	31,518	Sq.Ft.	$12,607,172	Nonrecurring
Total Nonrecurring Impact			$462,928,867				$755,484,758	
Total Nonrecurring Impact Per Capita			$17,822				$19,122	

	POPULATION & JOB METRICS		
Resident Population	25,975		39,509
Additional Temporary Population	12,650		23,527
Construction Jobs	81,487		125,854
Office Jobs	7,732		13,534
Retail Jobs	547		1,110

	CITY & STATE ANNUAL TAX REVENUE, ($) 2012			
Property	$253	Million	$399	Million
Sales	$83	Million	$143	Million
Employment	$53	Million	$94	Million
TOTAL	$389	Million	$636	Million

QUEENS BOULEVARD

SCENARIO 01

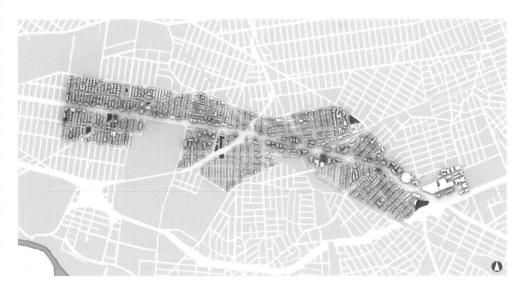

QUEENS BOULEVARD

SCENARIO 02

Office
Retail
Residential

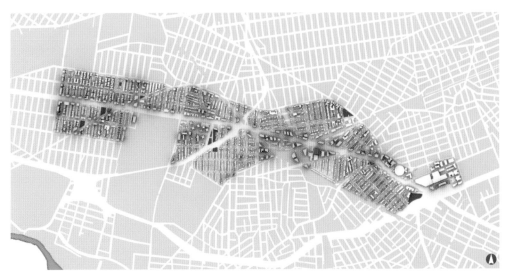

SCENARIO 01   SCENARIO 02

WALK SCORE

5   4   3   2   1

0-2 min 2-5 min 5-8 min 8-10 min 12-15 min

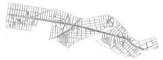

SKY EXPOSURE

0%   100%

BUILDING HEIGHTS

0   125'   250'   375'   500'

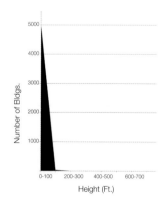
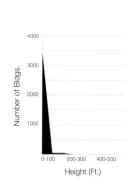

CURE. NYC 2040

QUEENS BOULEVARD

URBAN BENCHMARKING

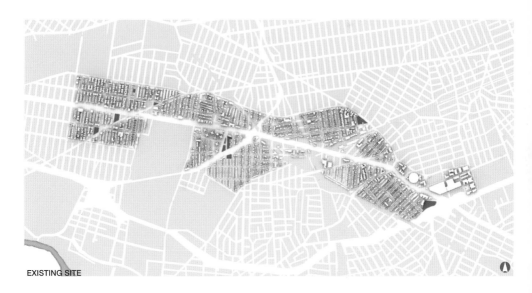

EXISTING SITE

AVERAGE OF MANHATTAN
SAMPLE CATCHMENT AREAS

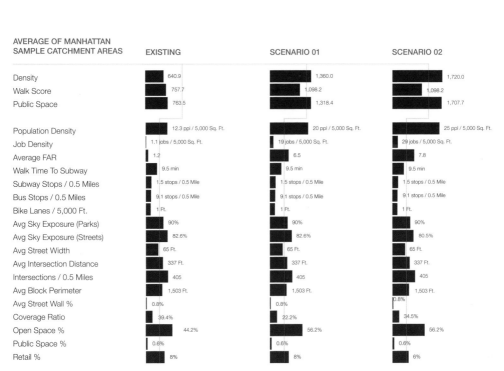

	EXISTING	SCENARIO 01	SCENARIO 02
Density	640.9	1,360.0	1,720.0
Walk Score	757.7	1,098.2	1,098.2
Public Space	763.5	1,318.4	1,707.7
Population Density	12.3 ppl / 5,000 Sq. Ft.	20 ppl / 5,000 Sq. Ft.	25 ppl / 5,000 Sq. Ft.
Job Density	1.1 jobs / 5,000 Sq. Ft.	19 jobs / 5,000 Sq. Ft.	29 jobs / 5,000 Sq. Ft.
Average FAR	1.2	6.5	7.8
Walk Time To Subway	9.5 min	9.5 min	9.5 min
Subway Stops / 0.5 Miles	1.5 stops / 0.5 Mile	1.5 stops / 0.5 Mile	1.5 stops / 0.5 Mile
Bus Stops / 0.5 Miles	9.1 stops / 0.5 Mile	9.1 stops / 0.5 Mile	9.1 stops / 0.5 Mile
Bike Lanes / 5,000 Ft.	1 Ft.	1 Ft.	1 Ft.
Avg Sky Exposure (Parks)	90%	90%	90%
Avg Sky Exposure (Streets)	82.6%	82.6%	80.5%
Avg Street Width	65 Ft.	65 Ft.	65 Ft.
Avg Intersection Distance	337 Ft.	337 Ft.	337 Ft.
Intersections / 0.5 Miles	405	405	405
Avg Block Perimeter	1,503 Ft.	1,503 Ft.	1,503 Ft.
Avg Street Wall %	0.8%	0.8%	0.8%
Coverage Ratio	39.4%	22.2%	34.5%
Open Space %	44.2%	56.2%	56.2%
Public Space %	0.6%	0.6%	0.6%
Retail %	8%	8%	6%

WILLETS POINT

SIMULATION RESULTS

	SCENARIO 01			SCENARIO 02		
	DEVELOPMENT METRICS					
	($) 2012	(FV) 2040 @ 3%	(PV) 2040 @ 10%	($) 2012	(FV) 2040 @ 3%	(PV) 2040 @ 10%
Total Development Cost				$5.65	$8.62 Billion	$1.87 Billion
Total Equity				$1.69	$2.59 Billion	$0.56 Billion
Total Market Value				$8.46	$12.97 Billion	$2.81 Billion
Total FAR of New Development				7.1		
Total Square Feet (Sq. Ft.)	7,400,000			11,306,624		
Total Residential Sq. Ft.	5,500,000	* Simulation Not Applicable;		8,776,676		
Total Office Sq. Ft.	4,228	Based on Actual Megaproject.		1,067,232		
Total Retail Sq. Ft.	500,000			1,462,716		
Total Residential Units	1,400,000			6,746		
Cost	$4.44 Billion					
Value	$5.75 Billion					

	IMPACT METRICS					
Facility	Service Estimate	Add't Service Cost		Service Estimate	Add't Service Cost	
Parks and Recreation				137	Acres	$14,375,035	Annual
Police				229	Officers	$25,408,491	Annual
Fire/Emergency Medical				104	Officers	$9,364,309	Annual
Water				5,476,204	Gallons	$9,994,072	Annual
Sewer				4,107,153	Gallons	$14,991,108	Annual
Schools				2,429	Students	$53,429,111	Annual
Total Annual Impact	* Simulation Not Applicable;				$127,562,127	
Total Annual Impact Per Capita	Based on Actual Megaproject.				$7,296	
Stormwater				18,892,903	Sq.Ft.	$623,465,815	Nonrecurring
Public Buildings				27,381	Sq.Ft.	$8,214,306	Nonrecurring
Courts and Justice				27,381	Sq.Ft.	$13,690,510	Nonrecurring
Libraries				27,381	Sq.Ft.	$10,952,408	Nonrecurring
Total Nonrecurring Impact					$656,323,038	
Total Nonrecurring Impact Per Capita					$37,540	

	POPULATION & JOB METRICS	
Resident Population		17,483
Additional Temporary Population		37,279
Construction Jobs	* Simulation Not Applicable;	56,043
Office Jobs	Based on Actual Megaproject.	8,024
Retail Jobs		3,250

	CITY & STATE ANNUAL TAX REVENUE, ($) 2012		
Property		$242	Million
Sales	* Simulation Not Applicable;	$229	Million
Employment	Based on Actual Megaproject.	$61	Million
TOTAL		$532	Million

WILLETS POINT
SCENARIO 01

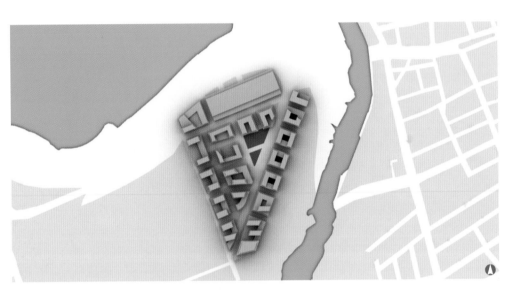

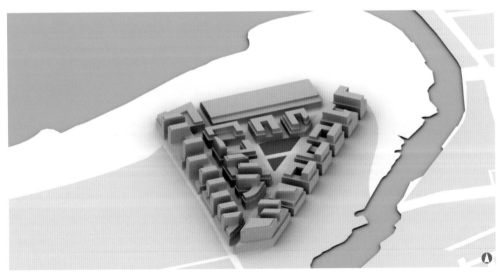

WILLETS POINT

SCENARIO 02

- Office
- Retail
- Residential

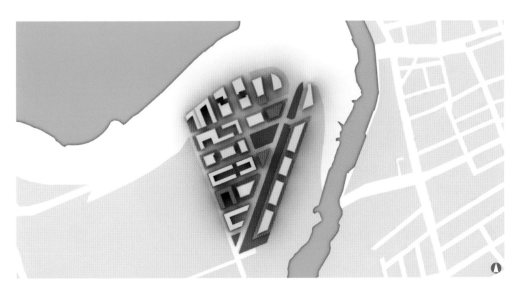

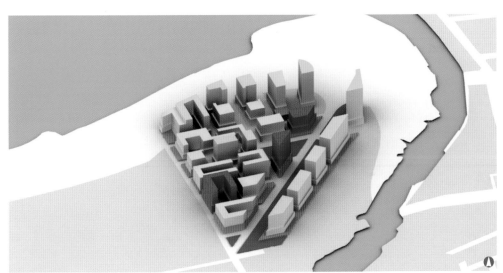

SCENARIO 01   SCENARIO 02

WALK SCORE

5	4	3	2	1
0-2 min	2-5 min	5-8 min	8-10 min	12-15 min

SKY EXPOSURE

0%   100%

BUILDING HEIGHTS

0	125'	250'	375'	500'

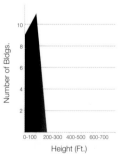 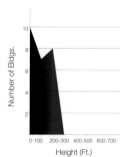

CURE. NYC 2040

WILLETS POINT

URBAN BENCHMARKING

EXISTING SITE

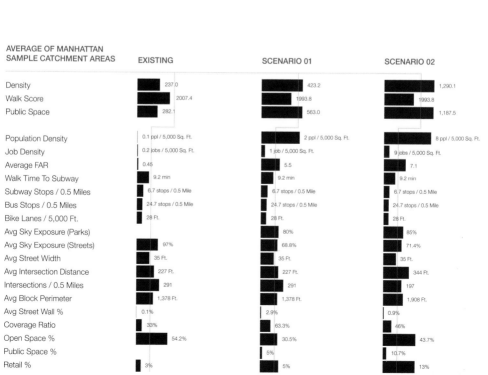

AVERAGE OF MANHATTAN SAMPLE CATCHMENT AREAS	EXISTING	SCENARIO 01	SCENARIO 02
Density	237.0	423.2	1,290.1
Walk Score	2007.4	1993.8	1993.8
Public Space	282.1	563.0	1,187.5
Population Density	0.1 ppl / 5,000 Sq. Ft.	2 ppl / 5,000 Sq. Ft.	8 ppl / 5,000 Sq. Ft.
Job Density	0.2 jobs / 5,000 Sq. Ft.	1 job / 5,000 Sq. Ft.	9 jobs / 5,000 Sq. Ft.
Average FAR	0.45	5.5	7.1
Walk Time To Subway	9.2 min	9.2 min	9.2 min
Subway Stops / 0.5 Miles	6.7 stops / 0.5 Mile	6.7 stops / 0.5 Mile	6.7 stops / 0.5 Mile
Bus Stops / 0.5 Miles	24.7 stops / 0.5 Mile	24.7 stops / 0.5 Mile	24.7 stops / 0.5 Mile
Bike Lanes / 5,000 Ft.	28 Ft.	28 Ft.	28 Ft.
Avg Sky Exposure (Parks)		80%	85%
Avg Sky Exposure (Streets)	97%	68.8%	71.4%
Avg Street Width	35 Ft.	35 Ft.	35 Ft.
Avg Intersection Distance	227 Ft.	227 Ft.	344 Ft.
Intersections / 0.5 Miles	291	291	197
Avg Block Perimeter	1,378 Ft.	1,378 Ft.	1,908 Ft.
Avg Street Wall %	0.1%	2.9%	0.9%
Coverage Ratio	33%	63.3%	46%
Open Space %	54.2%	30.5%	43.7%
Public Space %		5%	10.7%
Retail %	3%	5%	13%

VI. BROOKLYN

RED HOOK

BROOKLYN WATERFRONT

DOWNTOWN BROOKLYN

ATLANTIC YARDS

ATLANTIC AVENUE

0.5 1 2 mi

BROOKLYN AVAILABLE FAR [SQ. FT.]

Total Avail GFA	841,402,445
Total Avail Resi	279,855,836
Total Avail Comm	66,862,799
Total Avail Mixed	35,755,967
Total Avail Vacant	99,786,352

> 7.10
5.10 - 7.00
3.10 - 5.00
1.10 - 3.00
0.00 - 1.00

0.5   1   2 mi

CURE. NYC 2040

BROOKLYN DEVELOPMENT INDEX*

Total Avail GFA	116,201,698
Total Avail Resi	170,216
Total Avail Comm	7,435,853
Total Avail Mixed	-
Total Avail Vacant	51,826,886

■ 0.60 - 1.00
░ 0.30 - 0.59
▨ 0.00 - 0.29

*Areas taken from lots with scores of 0.60 or higher.

ATLANTIC AVENUE
SIMULATION RESULTS

	SCENARIO 01			SCENARIO 02		
DEVELOPMENT METRICS						
	($) 2012	(FV) 2040 @ 3%	(PV) 2040 @ 10%	($) 2012	(FV) 2040 @ 3%	(PV) 2040 @ 10%
Total Development Cost	$5.58	$8.55 Billion	$1.85 Billion	$8.33	$12.77 Billion	$2.76 Billion
Total Equity	$1.67	$2.56 Billion	$0.55 Billion	$2.49	$3.81 Billion	$0.82 Billion
Total Market Value	$7.59	$11.63 Billion	$2.52 Billion	$11.36	$17.41 Billion	$3.77 Billion
Total FAR of New Development	6.00			7.61		
Total Square Feet (Sq. Ft.)	11,166,785			16,663,441		
Total Residential Sq. Ft.	10,661,703			15,900,205		
Total Office Sq. Ft.	298,292			377,870		
Total Retail Sq. Ft.	206,790			385,366		
Total Residential Units	8,195			12,222		

IMPACT METRICS						
Facility	Service Estimate		Add't Service Cost		Service Estimate		Add't Service Cost	

Facility	Service Estimate		Add't Service Cost		Service Estimate		Add't Service Cost	
Parks and Recreation	69	Acres	$7,249,475	Annual	106	Acres	$11,083,318	Annual
Police	115	Officers	$12,813,758	Annual	176	Officers	$19,590,239	Annual
Fire/Emergency Medical	52	Officers	$4,722,515	Annual	80	Officers	$7,219,990	Annual
Water	2,761,705	Gallons	$5,040,111	Annual	4,222,216	Gallons	$7,705,545	Annual
Sewer	2,071,279	Gallons	$7,560,167	Annual	3,166,662	Gallons	$11,558,317	Annual
Schools	2,950	Students	$64,904,449	Annual	4,400	Students	$96,794,484	Annual
Total Annual Impact			$102,290,477				$153,951,893	
Total Annual Impact Per Capita			$4,816				$4,861	
Stormwater	9,527,882	Sq.Ft.	$314,420,105	Nonrecurring	14,566,646	Sq.Ft.	$480,699,325	Nonrecurring
Public Buildings	13,809	Sq.Ft.	$4,142,557	Nonrecurring	21,111	Sq.Ft.	$6,333,324	Nonrecurring
Courts and Justice	13,809	Sq.Ft.	$6,904,262	Nonrecurring	21,111	Sq.Ft.	$10,555,541	Nonrecurring
Libraries	13,809	Sq.Ft.	$5,523,410	Nonrecurring	21,111	Sq.Ft.	$8,444,433	Nonrecurring
Total Nonrecurring Impact			$330,990,334				$506,032,623	
Total Nonrecurring Impact Per Capita			$15,584				$15,976	

POPULATION & JOB METRICS		
Resident Population	21,238	31,674
Additional Temporary Population	6,379	10,548
Construction Jobs	63,178	94,017
Office Jobs	2,243	2,841
Retail Jobs	460	856

CITY & STATE ANNUAL TAX REVENUE, ($) 2012				
Property	$191	Million	$286	Million
Sales	$68	Million	$111	Million
Employment	$16	Million	$21	Million
TOTAL	$275	Million	$418	Million

ATLANTIC AVENUE

SCENARIO 01

ATLANTIC AVENUE

SCENARIO 02

Office
Retail
Residential

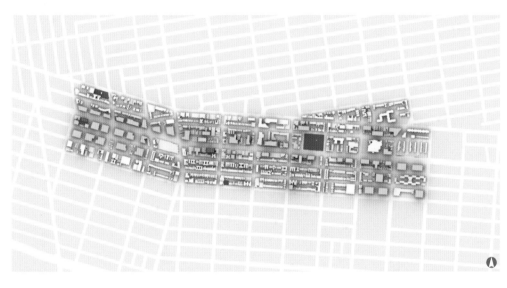

SCENARIO 01

SCENARIO 02

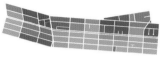

WALK SCORE

5	4	3	2	1
0-2 min	2-5 min	5-8 min	8-10 min	12-15 min

SKY EXPOSURE

0%   100%

BUILDING HEIGHTS

0   125'   250'   375'   500'

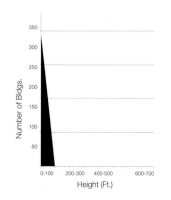
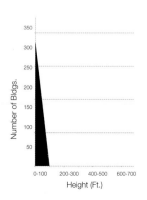

ATLANTIC AVENUE

URBAN BENCHMARKING

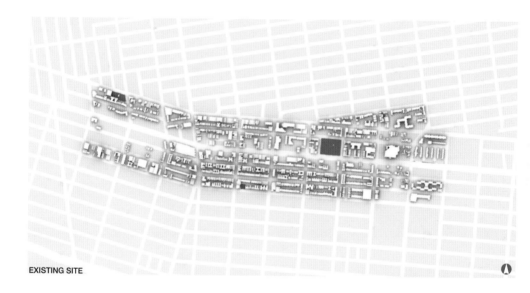

EXISTING SITE

AVERAGE OF MANHATTAN
SAMPLE CATCHMENT AREAS

	EXISTING	SCENARIO 01	SCENARIO 02
Density	679.0	1,190.5	1,448.0
Walk Score	1050.6	1,098.6	1,107.1
Public Space	766.2	1,128.5	1,347.3
Population Density	5.1 ppl / 5,000 Sq. Ft.	11 ppl / 5,000 Sq. Ft.	14 ppl / 5,000 Sq. Ft.
Job Density	4.6 jobs / 5,000 Sq. Ft.	18 jobs / 5,000 Sq. Ft.	24 jobs / 5,000 Sq. Ft.
Average FAR	1.7	6	7.6
Walk Time To Subway	6.6 min	6.6 min	6.6 min
Subway Stops / 0.5 Miles	3.1 stops / 0.5 Mile	3.1 stops / 0.5 Mile	3.1 stops / 0.5 Mile
Bus Stops / 0.5 Miles	18.3 stops / 0.5 Mile	18.3 stops / 0.5 Mile	18.3 stops / 0.5 Mile
Bike Lanes / 5,000 Ft.	9 Ft.	9 Ft.	9 Ft.
Avg Sky Exposure (Parks)	96%	95%	95%
Avg Sky Exposure (Streets)	87.6%	87.6%	85.3%
Avg Street Width	42 Ft.	42 Ft.	42 Ft.
Avg Intersection Distance	469 Ft.	469 Ft.	469 Ft.
Intersections / 0.5 Miles	271	271	271
Avg Block Perimeter	1,912 Ft.	1,912 Ft.	1,912 Ft.
Avg Street Wall %	0.4%	0.3%	0.3%
Coverage Ratio	43.7%	47.7%	47.7%
Open Space %	44.3%	44.3%	44.3%
Public Space %	1.4%	1.4%	1.4%
Retail %	8%	6%	6%

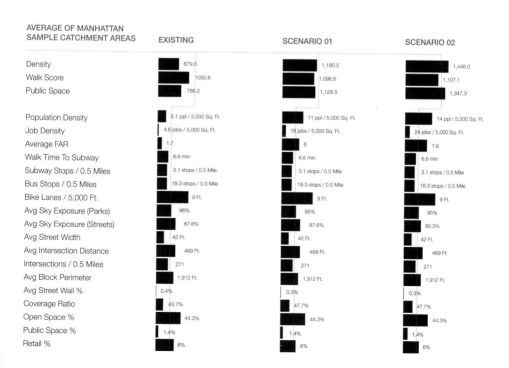

ATLANTIC YARDS

SIMULATION RESULTS

	SCENARIO 01			SCENARIO 02		
	DEVELOPMENT METRICS					
	($) 2012	(FV) 2040 @ 3%	(PV) 2040 @ 10%	($) 2012	(FV) 2040 @ 3%	(PV) 2040 @ 10%
Total Development Cost				$6.46	$9.90 Billion	$2.14 Billion
Total Equity				$1.93	$2.95 Billion	$0.64 Billion
Total Market Value				$8.87	$13.59 Billion	$2.94 Billion
Total FAR of New Development				10.03		
Total Square Feet (Sq. Ft.)	6,983,000	* Simulation Not Applicable; Based on Actual Megaproject.		12,929,389		
Total Residential Sq. Ft.	6,400,000			11,999,965		
Total Office Sq. Ft.	4,919			599,998		
Total Retail Sq. Ft.	336,000			329,426		
Total Residential Units	247,000			9,224		
Cost	$3.49 Billion					
Value	$4.83 Billion					

	IMPACT METRICS					
Facility	Service Estimate		Add't Service Cost	Service Estimate		Add't Service Cost
Parks and Recreation				88	Acres	$9,188,575	Annual
Police				146	Officers	$16,241,200	Annual
Fire/Emergency Medical				67	Officers	$5,985,700	Annual
Water				3,500,410	Gallons	$6,388,248	Annual
Sewer				2,625,307	Gallons	$9,582,371	Annual
Schools				3,321	Students	$73,051,286	Annual
Total Annual Impact	* Simulation Not Applicable; Based on Actual Megaproject.					$120,437,381
Total Annual Impact Per Capita						$5,038
Stormwater				12,076,413	Sq.Ft.	$398,521,632	Nonrecurring
Public Buildings				17,502	Sq.Ft.	$5,250,614	Nonrecurring
Courts and Justice				17,502	Sq.Ft.	$8,751,024	Nonrecurring
Libraries				17,502	Sq.Ft.	$7,000,819	Nonrecurring
Total Nonrecurring Impact						$419,524,089
Total Nonrecurring Impact Per Capita						$17,550

	POPULATION & JOB METRICS	
Resident Population		23,904
Additional Temporary Population	* Simulation Not Applicable; Based on Actual Megaproject.	11,100
Construction Jobs		72,713
Office Jobs		4,511
Retail Jobs		732

	CITY & STATE ANNUAL TAX REVENUE, ($) 2012		
Property		$227	Million
Sales	* Simulation Not Applicable;	$89	Million
Employment	Based on Actual Megaproject.	$32	Million
TOTAL		$348	Million

ATLANTIC YARDS

SCENARIO 01

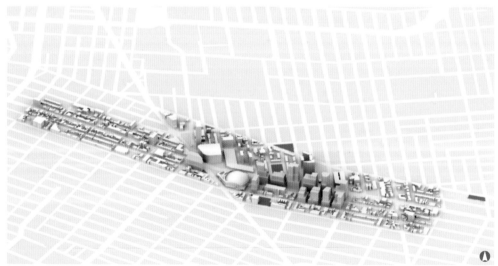

ATLANTIC YARDS

SCENARIO 02

Office
Retail
Residential

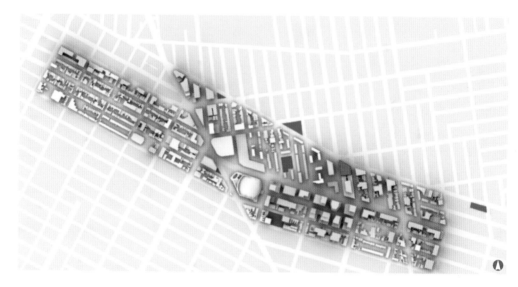

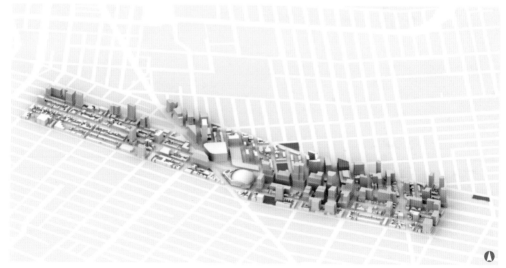

SCENARIO 01

SCENARIO 02

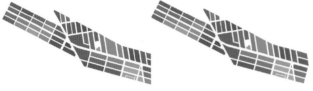

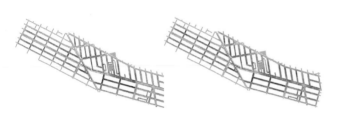

WALK SCORE

5	4	3	2	1
0-2 min	2-5 min	5-8 min	8-10 min	12-15 min

SKY EXPOSURE

0% — 100%

BUILDING HEIGHTS

0   125'   250'   375'   500'

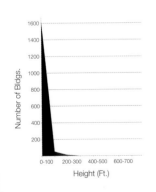

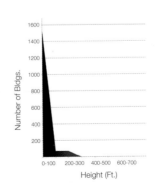

CURE. NYC 2040

ATLANTIC YARDS

URBAN BENCHMARKING

EXISTING SITE

AVERAGE OF MANHATTAN SAMPLE CATCHMENT AREAS	EXISTING	SCENARIO 01	SCENARIO 02
Density	647.5	1,192.5	1,588.2
Walk Score	1,559.2	1,569.9	1,559.2
Public Space	709.8	1,029.1	1,361.9
Population Density	3 ppl / 5,000 Sq. Ft.	6 ppl / 5,000 Sq. Ft.	10 ppl / 5,000 Sq. Ft.
Job Density	5 jobs / 5,000 Sq. Ft.	20 jobs / 5,000 Sq. Ft.	21 jobs / 5,000 Sq. Ft.
Average FAR	7.6	7.6	10
Walk Time To Subway	4.9 min	4.9 min	4.9 min
Subway Stops / 0.5 Miles	6.7 stops / 0.5 Mile	6.7 stops / 0.5 Mile	6.7 stops / 0.5 Mile
Bus Stops / 0.5 Miles	33.7 stops / 0.5 Mile	33.7 stops / 0.5 Mile	33.7 stops / 0.5 Mile
Bike Lanes / 5,000 Ft.	9 Ft.	9 Ft.	9 Ft.
Avg Sky Exposure (Parks)	90%	90%	90%
Avg Sky Exposure (Streets)	81%	81%	81%
Avg Street Width	58 Ft.	58 Ft.	58 Ft.
Avg Intersection Distance	133 Ft.	133 Ft.	133 Ft.
Intersections / 0.5 Miles	679	679	679
Avg Block Perimeter	1,580 Ft.	1,580 Ft.	1,580 Ft.
Avg Street Wall %	0.7%	0.7%	0.8%
Coverage Ratio	48.7%	48.7%	48.7%
Open Space %	75.2%	25.5%	25.5%
Public Space %	1%	1%	1%
Retail %	8%	8%	7%

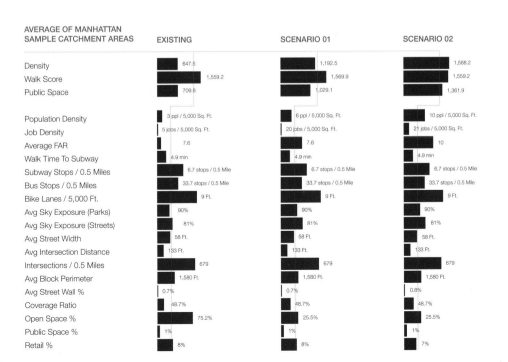

BROOKLYN WATERFRONT

SIMULATION RESULTS

	SCENARIO 01			SCENARIO 02		
DEVELOPMENT METRICS						
	($) 2012	(FV) 2040 @ 3%	(PV) 2040 @ 10%	($) 2012	(FV) 2040 @ 3%	(PV) 2040 @ 10%
Total Development Cost	$3.07	$4.70 Billion	$1.02 Billion	$7.64	$11.71 Billion	$2.53 Billion
Total Equity	$0.92	$1.41 Billion	$0.30 Billion	$2.29	$3.51 Billion	$0.76 Billion
Total Market Value	$3.79	$5.81 Billion	$1.25 Billion	$9.65	$14.79 Billion	$3.20 Billion
Total FAR of New Development	12.82			8.51		
Total Square Feet (Sq. Ft.)	5,155,226			12,733,650		
Total Residential Sq. Ft.	4,740,112			11,612,128		
Total Office Sq. Ft.	287,535			287,535		
Total Retail Sq. Ft.	105,431			833,987		
Total Residential Units	3,643			8,926		

IMPACT METRICS						
Facility	Service Estimate		Add't Service Cost	Service Estimate		Add't Service Cost
Parks and Recreation	35	Acres	$3,622,916	Annual	105	Acres	$11,018,014	Annual
Police	58	Officers	$6,403,659	Annual	175	Officers	$19,474,812	Annual
Fire/Emergency Medical	26	Officers	$2,360,071	Annual	80	Officers	$7,177,449	Annual
Water	1,380,158	Gallons	$2,518,789	Annual	4,197,339	Gallons	$20,986,693	Annual
Sewer	1,035,119	Gallons	$3,778,183	Annual	3,148,004	Gallons	$31,480,040	Annual
Schools	1,312	Students	$28,856,024	Annual	3,213	Students	$70,690,280	Annual
Total Annual Impact			$47,539,641				$160,827,287	
Total Annual Impact Per Capita			$5,035				$6,953	
Stormwater	4,761,546	Sq.Ft.	$157,131,028	Nonrecurring	14,480,818	Sq.Ft.	$477,867,004	Nonrecurring
Public Buildings	6,901	Sq.Ft.	$2,070,238	Nonrecurring	20,987	Sq.Ft.	$6,296,008	Nonrecurring
Courts and Justice	6,901	Sq.Ft.	$3,450,396	Nonrecurring	20,987	Sq.Ft.	$10,493,347	Nonrecurring
Libraries	6,901	Sq.Ft.	$2,760,317	Nonrecurring	20,987	Sq.Ft.	$8,394,677	Nonrecurring
Total Nonrecurring Impact			$165,411,978				$503,051,036	
Total Nonrecurring Impact Per Capita			$17,518				$21,747	

POPULATION & JOB METRICS		
Resident Population	9,442	23,132
Additional Temporary Population	4,359	18,842
Construction Jobs	29,035	71,198
Office Jobs	2,162	2,162
Retail Jobs	234	1,853

CITY & STATE ANNUAL TAX REVENUE, ($) 2012				
Property	$97	Million	$252	Million
Sales	$32	Million	$155	Million
Employment	$15	Million	$18	Million
TOTAL	$144	Million	$425	Million

BROOKLYN WATERFRONT
SCENARIO 01

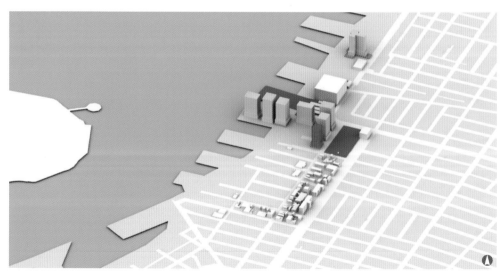

BROOKLYN WATERFRONT
SCENARIO 02

Office
Retail
Residential

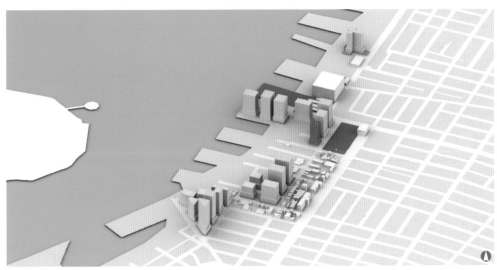

SCENARIO 01   SCENARIO 02

WALK SCORE

5	4	3	2	1
0-2 min	2-5 min	5-8 min	8-10 min	12-15 min

SKY EXPOSURE

0%   100%

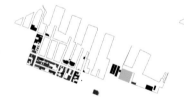 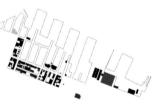

BUILDING HEIGHTS

0	125'	250'	375'	500'

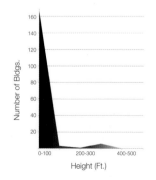 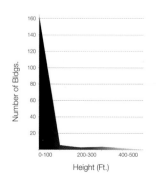

BROOKLYN WATERFRONT

URBAN BENCHMARKING

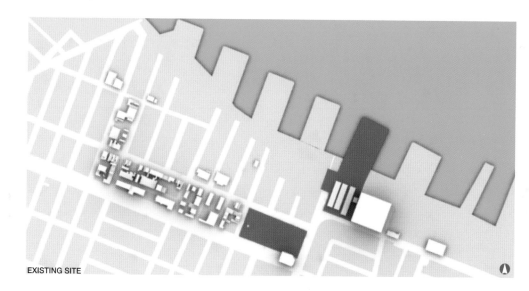

EXISTING SITE

AVERAGE OF MANHATTAN
SAMPLE CATCHMENT AREAS

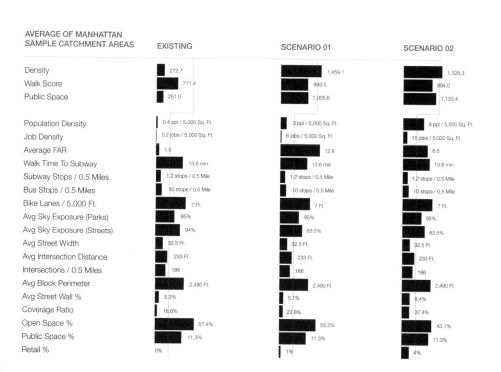

	EXISTING	SCENARIO 01	SCENARIO 02
Density	272.7	1,459.1	1,328.3
Walk Score	711.4	993.5	994.0
Public Space	251.0	1,005.6	1,133.4
Population Density	0.4 ppl / 5,000 Sq. Ft.	3 ppl / 5,000 Sq. Ft.	9 ppl / 5,000 Sq. Ft.
Job Density	0.2 jobs / 5,000 Sq. Ft.	6 jobs / 5,000 Sq. Ft.	15 jobs / 5,000 Sq. Ft.
Average FAR	1.5	12.8	8.5
Walk Time To Subway	13.6 min	13.6 min	13.6 min
Subway Stops / 0.5 Miles	1.2 stops / 0.5 Mile	1.2 stops / 0.5 Mile	1.2 stops / 0.5 Mile
Bus Stops / 0.5 Miles	10 stops / 0.5 Mile	10 stops / 0.5 Mile	10 stops / 0.5 Mile
Bike Lanes / 5,000 Ft.	7 Ft.	7 Ft.	7 Ft.
Avg Sky Exposure (Parks)	95%	95%	95%
Avg Sky Exposure (Streets)	94%	83.5%	83.5%
Avg Street Width	32.5 Ft.	32.5 Ft.	32.5 Ft.
Avg Intersection Distance	233 Ft.	233 Ft.	233 Ft.
Intersections / 0.5 Miles	186	186	186
Avg Block Perimeter	2,490 Ft.	2,490 Ft.	2,490 Ft.
Avg Street Wall %	5.3%	5.1%	8.4%
Coverage Ratio	16.6%	22.8%	37.4%
Open Space %	57.4%	53.2%	43.1%
Public Space %	11.3%	11.3%	11.3%
Retail %	0%	1%	4%

DOWNTOWN BROOKLYN

SIMULATION RESULTS

	SCENARIO 01			SCENARIO 02		
	DEVELOPMENT METRICS					
	($) 2012	(FV) 2040 @ 3%	(PV) 2040 @ 10%	($) 2012	(FV) 2040 @ 3%	(PV) 2040 @ 10%
Total Development Cost	$6.55	$10.04 Billion	$2.17 Billion	$9.41	$14.42 Billion	$3.12 Billion
Total Equity	$1.96	$3.00 Billion	$0.65 Billion	$2.82	$4.32 Billion	$0.93 Billion
Total Market Value	$7.51	$11.51 Billion	$2.49 Billion	$10.72	$16.43 Billion	$3.56 Billion
Total FAR of New Development	14.35			15.87		
Total Square Feet (Sq. Ft.)	10,925,699			15,688,520		
Total Residential Sq. Ft.	9,739,993			14,433,123		
Total Office Sq. Ft.	978,021			978,021		
Total Retail Sq. Ft.	207,685			277,376		
Total Residential Units	7,487			11,094		

	IMPACT METRICS					
Facility	Service Estimate		Add't Service Cost	Service Estimate		Add't Service Cost
Parks and Recreation	77	Acres	$8,113,775	Annual	104	Acres	$10,933,729	Annual
Police	129	Officers	$14,341,444	Annual	174	Officers	$19,325,835	Annual
Fire/Emergency Medical	59	Officers	$5,285,545	Annual	79	Officers	$7,122,544	Annual
Water	3,090,962	Gallons	$5,641,005	Annual	4,165,230	Gallons	$7,601,545	Annual
Sewer	2,318,221	Gallons	$8,461,508	Annual	3,123,923	Gallons	$11,402,318	Annual
Schools	2,695	Students	$59,293,424	Annual	3,994	Students	$87,863,439	Annual
Total Annual Impact			$101,136,701				$144,249,410	
Total Annual Impact Per Capita			$5,213				$5,017	
Stormwater	10,663,818	Sq.Ft.	$351,905,999	Nonrecurring	14,370,044	Sq.Ft.	$474,211,463	Nonrecurring
Public Buildings	15,455	Sq.Ft.	$4,636,443	Nonrecurring	20,826	Sq.Ft.	$6,247,845	Nonrecurring
Courts and Justice	15,455	Sq.Ft.	$7,727,404	Nonrecurring	20,826	Sq.Ft.	$10,413,076	Nonrecurring
Libraries	15,455	Sq.Ft.	$6,181,924	Nonrecurring	20,826	Sq.Ft.	$8,330,460	Nonrecurring
Total Nonrecurring Impact			$370,451,770				$499,202,844	
Total Nonrecurring Impact Per Capita			$19,093				$17,363	

	POPULATION & JOB METRICS	
Resident Population	19,402	28,751
Additional Temporary Population	11,507	12,901
Construction Jobs	61,785	88,468
Office Jobs	7,354	7,354
Retail Jobs	462	616

	CITY & STATE ANNUAL TAX REVENUE, ($) 2012			
Property	$197	Million	$276	Million
Sales	$65	Million	$92	Million
Employment	$51	Million	$51	Million
TOTAL	$313	Million	$419	Million

DOWNTOWN BROOKLYN

SCENARIO 01

DOWNTOWN BROOKLYN

SCENARIO 02

SCENARIO 01

SCENARIO 02

WALK SCORE

5	4	3	2	1
0-2 min	2-5 min	5-8 min	8-10 min	12-15 min

SKY EXPOSURE

0% ———————————— 100%

BUILDING HEIGHTS

0   125'   250'   375'   500'

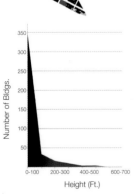

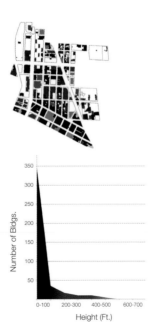

DOWNTOWN BROOKLYN

URBAN BENCHMARKING

EXISTING SITE

AVERAGE OF MANHATTAN SAMPLE CATCHMENT AREAS	EXISTING	SCENARIO 01	SCENARIO 02
Density	949.0	2,011.2	2,234.5
Walk Score	1210.5	1,214.3	1,207.5
Public Space	933.3	1,598.0	1,778.9
Population Density	2.8 ppl / 5,000 Sq. Ft.	9 ppl / 5,000 Sq. Ft.	11 ppl/5,000 Sq. Ft.
Job Density	17.7 jobs / 5,000 Sq. Ft.	32 jobs / 5,000 Sq. Ft.	37 jobs/5,000 Sq. Ft.
Average FAR	3.7	14.4	15.9
Walk Time To Subway	6 min	6 min	6 min
Subway Stops / 0.5 Miles	7 stops / 0.5 Mile	7 stops / 0.5 Mile	7 stops / 0.5 Mile
Bus Stops / 0.5 Miles	13.4 / 0.5 Mile	13.4 / 0.5 Mile	13.4 / 0.5 Mile
Bike Lanes / 5,000 Ft.	11 Ft.	11 Ft.	11 Ft.
Avg Sky Exposure (Parks)	90%	95%	95%
Avg Sky Exposure (Streets)	75%	69.4%	68.2%
Avg Street Width	62 ft	62 ft	62 Ft.
Avg Intersection Distance	154 ft	154 ft	154 Ft.
Intersections / 0.5 Miles	587	587	587
Avg Block Perimeter	1,379 Ft.	1,379 Ft.	1,379 Ft.
Avg Street Wall %	0.4%	0.4%	0.4%
Coverage Ratio	51.5%	48.1%	48.1%
Open Space %	24.5%	26.8%	26.8%
Public Space %	13.5%	13.5%	13.5%
Retail %	7%	6%	5%

RED HOOK
SIMULATION RESULTS

	SCENARIO 01			SCENARIO 02		
DEVELOPMENT METRICS						
	($) 2012	(FV) 2040 @ 3%	(PV) 2040 @ 10%	($) 2012	(FV) 2040 @ 3%	(PV) 2040 @ 10%
Total Development Cost	$6.32	$9.69 Billion	$2.10 Billion	$12.78	$19.59 Billion	$4.24 Billion
Total Equity	$1.89	$2.89 Billion	$0.62 Billion	$3.83	$5.87 Billion	$1.27 Billion
Total Market Value	$7.12	$10.91 Billion	$2.36 Billion	$14.53	$22.27 Billion	$4.82 Billion
Total FAR of New Development	5.13			5.51		
Total Square Feet (Sq. Ft.)	10,538,401			21,308,745		
Total Residential Sq. Ft.	10,345,653			20,691,462		
Total Office Sq. Ft.	0			0		
Total Retail Sq. Ft.	192,748			617,283		
Total Residential Units	7,952			15,904		

	IMPACT METRICS					
Facility	Service Estimate		Add't Service Cost		Service Estimate	Add't Service Cost
Parks and Recreation	61	Acres	$6,421,756	Annual	134	Acres	$14,060,474	Annual
Police	102	Officers	$11,350,728	Annual	224	Officers	$24,852,491	Annual
Fire/Emergency Medical	46	Officers	$4,183,315	Annual	102	Officers	$9,159,395	Annual
Water	2,446,383	Gallons	$4,464,649	Annual	5,356,371	Gallons	$9,775,377	Annual
Sewer	1,834,787	Gallons	$6,696,974	Annual	4,017,278	Gallons	$14,663,066	Annual
Schools	2,863	Students	$62,980,455	Annual	5,726	Students	$125,961,859	Annual
Total Annual Impact			$96,097,876				$198,472,663	
Total Annual Impact Per Capita			$4,663				$4,815	
Stormwater	8,440,022	Sq.Ft.	$278,520,710	Nonrecurring	18,479,481	Sq.Ft.	$609,822,859	Nonrecurring
Public Buildings	12,232	Sq.Ft.	$3,669,575	Nonrecurring	26,782	Sq.Ft.	$8,034,557	Nonrecurring
Courts and Justice	12,232	Sq.Ft.	$6,115,958	Nonrecurring	26,782	Sq.Ft.	$13,390,928	Nonrecurring
Libraries	12,232	Sq.Ft.	$4,892,766	Nonrecurring	26,782	Sq.Ft.	$10,712,742	Nonrecurring
Total Nonrecurring Impact			$293,199,009				$641,961,086	
Total Nonrecurring Impact Per Capita			$14,227				$15,575	

POPULATION & JOB METRICS		
Resident Population	20,609	41,218
Additional Temporary Population	3,855	12,346
Construction Jobs	59,078	119,255
Office Jobs	0	0
Retail Jobs	428	1,372

CITY & STATE ANNUAL TAX REVENUE, ($) 2012				
Property	$301	Million	$363	Million
Sales	$64	Million	$160	Million
Employment	$0.88	Million	$2.84	Million
TOTAL	$365.88	Million	$525.84	Million

RED HOOK

SCENARIO 01

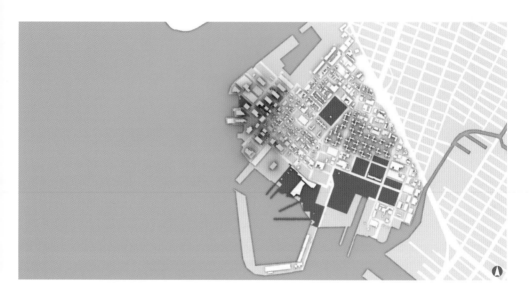

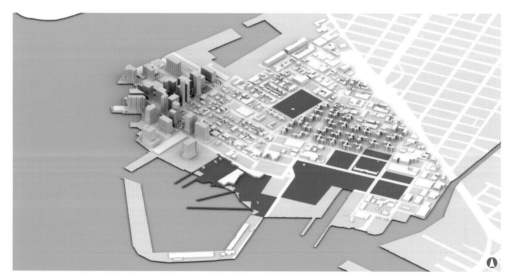

RED HOOK

SCENARIO 02

Office
Retail
Residential

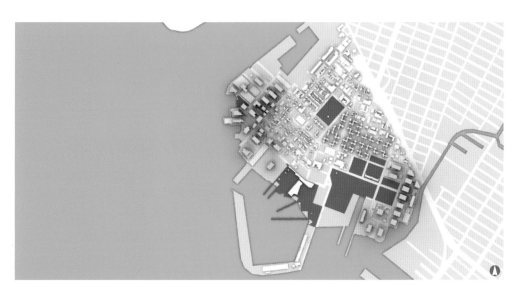

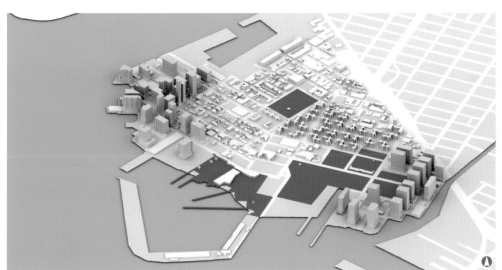

SCENARIO 01   SCENARIO 02

WALK SCORE

5	4	3	2	1
0-2 min	2-5 min	5-8 min	8-10 min	12-15 min

SKY EXPOSURE

0%   100%

BUILDING HEIGHTS

0	125'	250'	375'	500'

CURE. NYC 2040

RED HOOK

URBAN BENCHMARKING

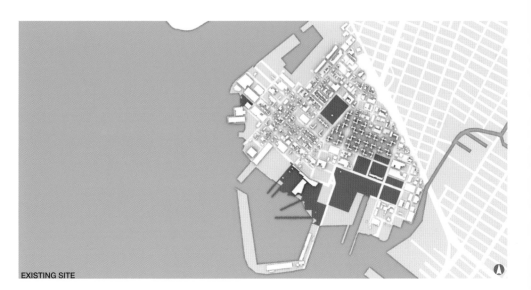

EXISTING SITE

AVERAGE OF MANHATTAN SAMPLE CATCHMENT AREAS	EXISTING	SCENARIO 01	SCENARIO 02
Density	1,353	1,525.6	1,773.3
Walk Score	912.6	900.9	900.9
Public Space	1717	1,646.1	1,932.4
Population Density	23 ppl / 5,000 Sq. Ft.	28 ppl / 5,000 Sq. Ft.	34 ppl / 5,000 Sq. Ft.
Job Density	0.5 jobs / 5,000 Sq. Ft.	12 jobs / 5,000 Sq. Ft.	25 jobs / 5,000 Sq. Ft.
Average FAR	1.2	5.1	5.5
Walk Time To Subway	13.4 min	13.4 min	13.4 min
Subway Stops / 0.5 Miles	.9 stops / 0.5 Mile	.9 stops / 0.5 Mile	.9 stops / 0.5 Mile
Bus Stops / 0.5 Miles	7.7 stops / 0.5 Mile	7.7 stops / 0.5 Mile	7.7 stops / 0.5 Mile
Bike Lanes / 5,000 Ft.	3 Ft.	3 Ft.	3 Ft.
Avg Sky Exposure (Parks)	95%	95%	95%
Avg Sky Exposure (Streets)	86.6%	86.6%	85.8%
Avg Street Width	33.7 Ft.	33.7 Ft.	33.7 Ft.
Avg Intersection Distance	319 Ft.	319 Ft.	319 Ft.
Intersections / 0.5 Miles	210	210	210
Avg Block Perimeter	1,351 Ft.	1,351 Ft.	1,351 Ft.
Avg Street Wall %	1.2%	1.2%	1.4%
Coverage Ratio	40.2%	45.2%	40.2%
Open Space %	67.8%	65.5%	67.8%
Public Space %	29.2%	29.2%	29.2%
Retail %	4%	4%	19%

VII. BRONX

SHERRIDAN EXPRESSWAY

SOUTH CONCOURSE

0.5 1 2 mi

BROOKLYN AVAILABLE FAR [SQ. FT.]

Total Avail GFA	643,562,509
Total Avail Resi	175,272,276
Total Avail Comm	59,593,856
Total Avail Mixed	15,796,882
Total Avail Vacant	53,427,390

- ■ > 7.10
- ▨ 5.10 - 7.00
- ▨ 3.10 - 5.00
- ▨ 1.10 - 3.00
- ■ 0.00 - 1.00

CURE. NYC 2040

BROOKLYN DEVELOPMENT INDEX*

Total Avail GFA	69,128,379
Total Avail Resi	6,002
Total Avail Comm	11,581,155
Total Avail Mixed	-
Total Avail Vacant	25,225,584

■ 0.60 - 1.00
□ 0.30 - 0.59
■ 0.00 - 0.29

*Areas taken from lots with scores of 0.60 or higher.

SHERIDAN EXPRESSWAY

SIMULATION RESULTS

	SCENARIO 01			SCENARIO 02		
DEVELOPMENT METRICS						
	($) 2012	(FV) 2040 @ 3%	(PV) 2040 @ 10%	($) 2012	(FV) 2040 @ 3%	(PV) 2040 @ 10%
Total Development Cost	$4.43	$6.79 Billion	$1.47 Billion	$6.54	$10.02 Billion	$2.17 Billion
Total Equity	$1.33	$2.03 Billion	$0.44 Billion	$1.96	$3.00 Billion	$0.65 Billion
Total Market Value	$5.29	$8.11 Billion	$1.75 Billion	$7.88	$12.08 Billion	$2.61 Billion
Total FAR of New Development	7.9			8.72		
Total Square Feet (Sq. Ft.)	11,091,752			16,350,234		
Total Residential Sq. Ft.	10,514,993			15,512,633		
Total Office Sq. Ft.	354,825			354,825		
Total Retail Sq. Ft.	221,934			482,776		
Total Residential Units	8,082			11,155		

			IMPACT METRICS					
Facility	Service Estimate		Add't Service Cost		Service Estimate		Add't Service Cost	
Parks and Recreation	70	Acres	$7,363,844	Annual	108	Acres	$11,346,572	Annual
Police	117	Officers	$13,015,910	Annual	181	Officers	$20,055,552	Annual
Fire/Emergency Medical	53	Officers	$4,797,018	Annual	82	Officers	$7,391,481	Annual
Water	2,805,274	Gallons	$5,119,625	Annual	4,322,504	Gallons	$7,888,569	Annual
Sewer	2,103,955	Gallons	$7,679,437	Annual	3,241,878	Gallons	$11,832,854	Annual
Schools	2,910	Students	$64,011,333	Annual	4,016	Students	$88,350,339	Annual
Total Annual Impact			$101,987,167				$146,865,368	
Total Annual Impact Per Capita			$4,869				$4,753	
Stormwater	9,678,195	Sq.Ft.	$319,380,426	Nonrecurring	14,912,638	Sq.Ft.	$492,117,041	Nonrecurring
Public Buildings	14,026	Sq.Ft.	$4,207,911	Nonrecurring	21,613	Sq.Ft.	$6,483,755	Nonrecurring
Courts and Justice	14,026	Sq.Ft.	$7,013,185	Nonrecurring	21,613	Sq.Ft.	$10,806,259	Nonrecurring
Libraries	14,026	Sq.Ft.	$5,610,548	Nonrecurring	21,613	Sq.Ft.	$8,645,007	Nonrecurring
Total Nonrecurring Impact			$336,212,069				$518,052,063	
Total Nonrecurring Impact Per Capita			$16,051				$16,765	

	POPULATION & JOB METRICS				
Resident Population	20,946			30,902	
Additional Temporary Population	7,107			12,323	
Construction Jobs	62,549			92,007	
Office Jobs	2,668			2,668	
Retail Jobs	493			1,073	

	CITY & STATE ANNUAL TAX REVENUE, ($) 2012				
Property	$143	Million	$201	Million	
Sales	$69	Million	$123	Million	
Employment	$19	Million	$20	Million	
TOTAL	$221	Million	$344	Million	

SHERIDAN EXPRESSWAY

SCENARIO 01

SHERIDAN EXPRESSWAY

SCENARIO 02

SCENARIO 01   SCENARIO 02

WALK SCORE

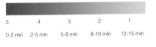

5	4	3	2	1
0-2 min	2-5 min	5-8 min	8-10 min	12-15 min

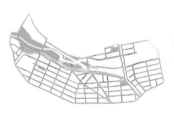

SKY EXPOSURE

0%   100%

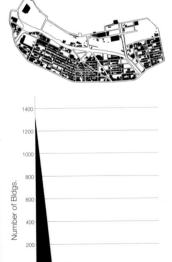

BUILDING HEIGHTS

0   125'   250'   375'   500'

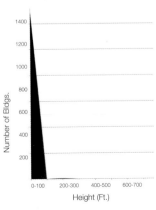

CURE. NYC 2040

SHERIDAN EXPRESSWAY
URBAN BENCHMARKING

EXISTING SITE

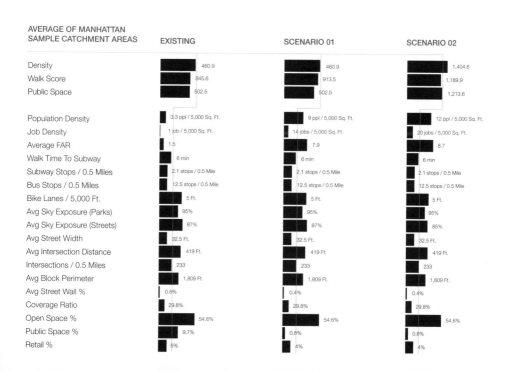

AVERAGE OF MANHATTAN SAMPLE CATCHMENT AREAS	EXISTING	SCENARIO 01	SCENARIO 02
Density	460.9	460.9	1,404.6
Walk Score	845.6	913.5	1,189.9
Public Space	502.5	502.5	1,213.6
Population Density	3.3 ppl / 5,000 Sq. Ft.	9 ppl / 5,000 Sq. Ft.	12 ppl / 5,000 Sq. Ft.
Job Density	1 job / 5,000 Sq. Ft.	14 jobs / 5,000 Sq. Ft.	20 jobs / 5,000 Sq. Ft.
Average FAR	1.5	7.9	8.7
Walk Time To Subway	6 min	6 min	6 min
Subway Stops / 0.5 Miles	2.1 stops / 0.5 Mile	2.1 stops / 0.5 Mile	2.1 stops / 0.5 Mile
Bus Stops / 0.5 Miles	12.5 stops / 0.5 Mile	12.5 stops / 0.5 Mile	12.5 stops / 0.5 Mile
Bike Lanes / 5,000 Ft.	5 Ft.	5 Ft.	5 Ft.
Avg Sky Exposure (Parks)	95%	95%	95%
Avg Sky Exposure (Streets)	87%	87%	85%
Avg Street Width	32.5 Ft.	32.5 Ft.	32.5 Ft.
Avg Intersection Distance	419 Ft.	419 Ft.	419 Ft.
Intersections / 0.5 Miles	233	233	233
Avg Block Perimeter	1,809 Ft.	1,809 Ft.	1,809 Ft.
Avg Street Wall %	0.5%	0.4%	0.4%
Coverage Ratio	29.8%	29.8%	29.8%
Open Space %	54.6%	54.6%	54.6%
Public Space %	9.7%	0.8%	0.8%
Retail %	5%	4%	4%

SOUTH CONCOURSE

SIMULATION RESULTS

	SCENARIO 01			SCENARIO 02		
DEVELOPMENT METRICS						
	($) 2012	(FV) 2040 @ 3%	(PV) 2040 @ 10%	($) 2012	(FV) 2040 @ 3%	(PV) 2040 @ 10%
Total Development Cost	$3.89	$5.96 Billion	$1.29	$7.47	$11.45 Billion	$2.48 Billion
Total Equity	$1.16	$1.77 Billion	$0.38	$2.24	$3.43 Billion	$0.74 Billion
Total Market Value	$4.65	$7.12 Billion	$1.54	$9.03	$13.84 Billion	$3.00 Billion
Total FAR of New Development	5.03			5.85		
Total Square Feet (Sq. Ft.)	9,749,926			18,684,792		
Total Residential Sq. Ft.	8,993,669			17,516,234		
Total Office Sq. Ft.	590,982			590,982		
Total Retail Sq. Ft.	165,275			577,576		
Total Residential Units	6,913			13,464		

	IMPACT METRICS							
Facility	Service Estimate		Add't Service Cost		Service Estimate		Add't Service Cost	
Parks and Recreation	64	Acres	$6,736,970	Annual	127	Acres	$13,358,071	Annual
Police	107	Officers	$11,907,884	Annual	213	Officers	$23,610,963	Annual
Fire/Emergency Medical	49	Officers	$4,388,655	Annual	97	Officers	$8,701,829	Annual
Water	2,566,465	Gallons	$4,683,798	Annual	5,088,789	Gallons	$9,287,040	Annual
Sewer	1,924,849	Gallons	$7,025,698	Annual	3,816,592	Gallons	$13,930,560	Annual
Schools	2,489	Students	$54,750,083	Annual	4,847	Students	$106,632,262	Annual
Total Annual Impact			$89,493,089				$175,520,726	
Total Annual Impact Per Capita			$4,995				$5,030	
Stormwater	8,854,304	Sq.Ft.	$292,192,029	Nonrecurring	17,556,322	Sq.Ft.	$579,358,629	Nonrecurring
Public Buildings	12,832	Sq.Ft.	$3,849,697	Nonrecurring	25,444	Sq.Ft.	$7,633,184	Nonrecurring
Courts and Justice	12,832	Sq.Ft.	$6,416,162	Nonrecurring	25,444	Sq.Ft.	$12,721,973	Nonrecurring
Libraries	12,832	Sq.Ft.	$5,132,930	Nonrecurring	25,444	Sq.Ft.	$10,177,578	Nonrecurring
Total Nonrecurring Impact			$307,590,818				$609,891,363	
Total Nonrecurring Impact Per Capita			$17,169				$17,479	

	POPULATION & JOB METRICS		
Resident Population	17,916		34,893
Additional Temporary Population	7,749		15,995
Construction Jobs	55,358		106,862
Office Jobs	4,443		4,443
Retail Jobs	367		1,284

	CITY & STATE ANNUAL TAX REVENUE, ($) 2012			
Property	$120	Million	$232	Million
Sales	$56	Million	$143	Million
Employment	$31	Million	$32	Million
TOTAL	$207	Million	$407	Million

SOUTH CONCOURSE

SCENARIO 01

SOUTH CONCOURSE

SCENARIO 02

■ Office
■ Retail
□ Residential

SCENARIO 01   SCENARIO 02

WALK SCORE

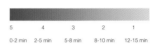

5	4	3	2	1
0-2 min	2-5 min	5-8 min	8-10 min	12-15 min

SKY EXPOSURE

0%_____100%

BUILDING HEIGHTS

0   125'   250'   375'   500'

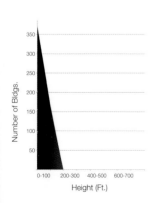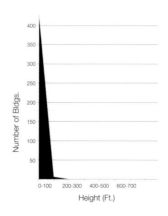

CURE. NYC 2040

SOUTH CONCOURSE

URBAN BENCHMARKING

EXISTING SITE

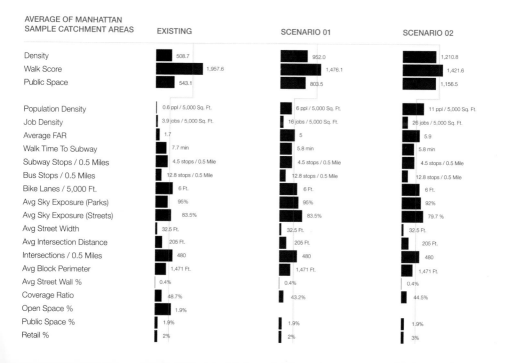

AVERAGE OF MANHATTAN
SAMPLE CATCHMENT AREAS

	EXISTING	SCENARIO 01	SCENARIO 02
Density	508.7	952.0	1,210.8
Walk Score	1,957.6	1,476.1	1,421.6
Public Space	543.1	803.5	1,156.5
Population Density	0.6 ppl / 5,000 Sq. Ft.	6 ppl / 5,000 Sq. Ft.	11 ppl / 5,000 Sq. Ft.
Job Density	3.9 jobs / 5,000 Sq. Ft.	16 jobs / 5,000 Sq. Ft.	26 jobs / 5,000 Sq. Ft.
Average FAR	1.7	5	5.9
Walk Time To Subway	7.7 min	5.8 min	5.8 min
Subway Stops / 0.5 Miles	4.5 stops / 0.5 Mile	4.5 stops / 0.5 Mile	4.5 stops / 0.5 Mile
Bus Stops / 0.5 Miles	12.8 stops / 0.5 Mile	12.8 stops / 0.5 Mile	12.8 stops / 0.5 Mile
Bike Lanes / 5,000 Ft.	6 Ft.	6 Ft.	6 Ft.
Avg Sky Exposure (Parks)	95%	95%	92%
Avg Sky Exposure (Streets)	83.5%	83.5%	79.7 %
Avg Street Width	32.5 Ft.	32.5 Ft.	32.5 Ft.
Avg Intersection Distance	205 Ft.	205 Ft.	205 Ft.
Intersections / 0.5 Miles	480	480	480
Avg Block Perimeter	1,471 Ft.	1,471 Ft.	1,471 Ft.
Avg Street Wall %	0.4%	0.4%	0.4%
Coverage Ratio	48.7%	43.2%	44.5%
Open Space %	1.9%		
Public Space %	1.9%	1.9%	1.9%
Retail %	2%	2%	3%

VIII. STATEN ISLAND

ST GEORGE / STAPLETON

0.5 1 2 mi

STATEN ISLAND AVAILABLE FAR [SQ. FT.]

Total Avail GFA	605,926,854
Total Avail Resi	95,118,336
Total Avail Comm	33,243,429
Total Avail Mixed	2,302,514
Total Avail Vacant	193,188,636

> 7.10
5.10 - 7.00
3.10 - 5.00
1.10 - 3.00
0.00 - 1.00

CURE. NYC 2040

STATEN ISLAND DEVELOPMENT INDEX*

Total Avail GFA	222,784,053
Total Avail Resi	1,387,717
Total Avail Comm	5,016,513
Total Avail Mixed	126,479
Total Avail Vacant	149,858,659

- ■ 0.60 - 1.00
- ■ 0.30 - 0.59
- ■ 0.00 - 0.29

*Areas taken from lots with scores of 0.60 or higher.

ST. GEORGE / STAPLETON
SIMULATION RESULTS

	SCENARIO 01			SCENARIO 02		
DEVELOPMENT METRICS						
	($) 2012	(FV) 2040 @ 3%	(PV) 2040 @ 10%	($) 2012	(FV) 2040 @ 3%	(PV) 2040 @ 10%
Total Development Cost	$2.85	$4.36	$0.94	$6.48	$9.93	$2.15
Total Equity	$0.86	$1.31	$0.28	$1.94	$2.97	$0.64
Total Market Value	$3.39	$5.19	$1.12	$7.79	$11.94	$2.58
Total FAR of New Development	9.18			8.24		
Total Square Feet (Sq. Ft.)	7,130,940			16,216,816		
Total Residential Sq. Ft.	6,591,424			15,346,637		
Total Office Sq. Ft.	433,258			433,258		
Total Retail Sq. Ft.	106,258			436,921		
Total Residential Units	5,066			11,796		

IMPACT METRICS						
Facility	Service Estimate		Add't Service Cost		Service Estimate	Add't Service Cost
Parks and Recreation	46	Acres	$4,859,680	Annual	106	Acres	$11,173,835	Annual
Police	77	Officers	$8,589,692	Annual	178	Officers	$19,750,232	Annual
Fire/Emergency Medical	35	Officers	$3,165,734	Annual	81	Officers	$7,278,955	Annual
Water	1,851,307	Gallons	$3,378,634	Annual	4,256,699	Gallons	$7,768,475	Annual
Sewer	1,388,480	Gallons	$5,067,952	Annual	3,192,524	Gallons	$11,652,713	Annual
Schools	1,824	Students	$40,126,117	Annual	4,247	Students	$93,424,570	Annual
Total Annual Impact			$65,187,809			$151,048,780	
Total Annual Impact Per Capita			$4,965			$4,941	
Stormwater	6,387,008	Sq.Ft.	$210,771,252	Nonrecurring	14,685,611	Sq.Ft.	$484,625,170	Nonrecurring
Public Buildings	9,257	Sq.Ft.	$2,776,960	Nonrecurring	21,283	Sq.Ft.	$6,385,048	Nonrecurring
Courts and Justice	9,257	Sq.Ft.	$4,628,266	Nonrecurring	21,283	Sq.Ft.	$10,641,747	Nonrecurring
Libraries	9,257	Sq.Ft.	$3,702,613	Nonrecurring	21,283	Sq.Ft.	$8,513,398	Nonrecurring
Total Nonrecurring Impact			$221,879,092			$510,165,363	
Total Nonrecurring Impact Per Capita			$16,898			$16,688	

POPULATION & JOB METRICS		
Resident Population	13,130	30,571
Additional Temporary Population	5,383	11,996
Construction Jobs	40,219	91,560
Office Jobs	3,258	3,258
Retail Jobs	236	971

CITY & STATE ANNUAL TAX REVENUE, ($) 2012				
Property	$87	Million	$199	Million
Sales	$39	Million	$116	Million
Employment	$22	Million	$24	Million
TOTAL	$148	Million	$339	Million

ST. GEORGE / STAPLETON

SCENARIO 01

ST. GEORGE / STAPLETON

SCENARIO 02

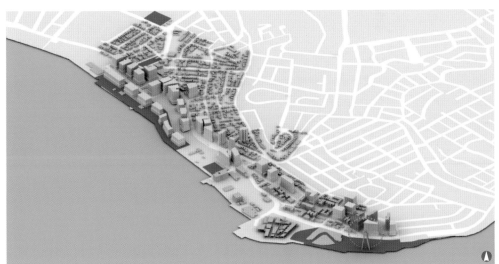

SCENARIO 01

SCENARIO 02

WALK SCORE

5	4	3	2	1
0-2 min	2-5 min	5-8 min	8-10 min	12-15 min

SKY EXPOSURE

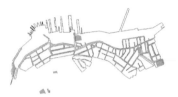

0%   100%

BUILDING HEIGHTS

0	125'	250'	375'	500'

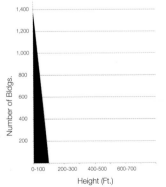
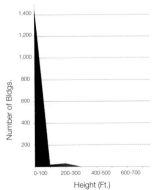

CURE. NYC 2040

ST. GEORGE / STAPLETON
URBAN BENCHMARKING

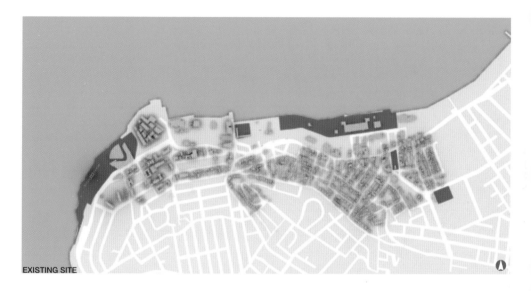

EXISTING SITE

AVERAGE OF MANHATTAN SAMPLE CATCHMENT AREAS	EXISTING	SCENARIO 01	SCENARIO 02
Density	284.2	952.0	1,210.8
Walk Score	965.0	1,476.1	1,421.6
Public Space	309.6	803.5	1,156.5
Population Density	1.6 ppl / 5,000 Sq. Ft.	6 ppl / 5,000 Sq. Ft.	11 ppl / 5,000 Sq. Ft.
Job Density	2.3 jobs / 5,000 Sq. Ft.	16 jobs / 5,000 Sq. Ft.	26 jobs / 5,000 Sq. Ft.
Average FAR	0.9	5	5.9
Walk Time To Subway	5.8 min	5.8 min	5.8 min
Subway Stops / 0.5 Miles	4.5 stops / 0.5 Mile	4.5 stops / 0.5 Mile	4.5 stops / 0.5 Mile
Bus Stops / 0.5 Miles	12.8 stops / 0.5 Mile	12.8 stops / 0.5 Mile	12.8 stops / 0.5 Mile
Bike Lanes / 5,000 Ft.	6 Ft.	6 Ft.	6 Ft.
Avg Sky Exposure (Parks)	96.5%	95%	92%
Avg Sky Exposure (Streets)	89%	83.5%	79.7 %
Avg Street Width	32.5 Ft.	32.5 Ft.	32.5 Ft.
Avg Intersection Distance	205 Ft.	205 Ft.	205 Ft.
Intersections / 0.5 Miles	480	480	480
Avg Block Perimeter	1,471 Ft.	1,471 Ft.	1,471 Ft.
Avg Street Wall %	0.4%	0.4%	0.4%
Coverage Ratio	21.9%	43.2%	44.5%
Open Space %	69.6%	0.0 %	0.0 %
Public Space %	3.1%	1.9%	1.9%
Retail %	7%	2%	3%

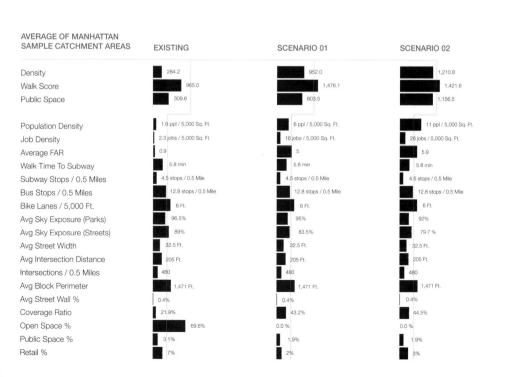

IX. CONCLUSIONS:
REINVESTING, NOT RETREATING

The public discourse surrounding notions of increased density is often clouded by the interests of stakeholders who may or may not have any actual interest in the future of the city beyond a generation or two. At the same time, a tension exists wherein cities need to plan for the infrastructure, including housing infrastructure, whose useful life and programmatic footprint often exceeds two or three generations. This latent tension serves as a drag on any democratizing institution whose conflicting mandates more often than not result in a fatally flawed incrementalism which costs more in the long-run. The counter point to this phenomenon is the kind of urban investment that is both over scaled, costly and socially disruptive.

Through the testing of hyper density in the subject zones, this report implicitly argues that reasonable investments can be in locations which already have the requisite capacity for increased density. Although, technically speaking, the hypothesis that the zones could handle the density failed in that they were only able to handle 94.66% of the projected space allocations under Scenario #1. An additional shortcoming of the results highlight the increased risk and difficulty of building scaled urban development when you are forced to build with Manhattan costs and outer borough revenues. However, to more intelligently distribute public and private resources to promote the development of the outer boroughs it will require strong political leadership which must be able to communicate the advantages and risks of such development.

By managing long-term infrastructure investment and short-term incremental development, the process of urban development can be managed in a way that is both respectful of the interests of the status quo and, in this case, the housing needs of future residents–many of whom may not ever be born yet. In more immediate terms, the abrupt housing crisis following Hurricane Sandy underscores the necessity to think of housing as a type of infrastructure which warrants public investment not just for the needy but for all New Yorkers who strive to find a decent place to live.

In the aftermath of Hurricane Sandy, the city must not retreat from the waterfront. Aside from the recreational and aesthetic implications, the waterfront is intrinsically linked to the history, culture and geography of NYC. This is not to mention that the waterfront in the outer boroughs is often the closest point of departure to the employments centers of Midtown Manhattan, the Financial District and Downtown Brooklyn. After all, preferencing proximity especially to mass transit is at the core of this report's simulation exercises.

However, the reemergence of the waterfront is not simply grounded in transportation logistics as the north-south axis from Red Hook to Long Island City already represents a parallel economic continuum which could once again rival that of Manhattan's east side. The alternative is an encroaching coastline and declining property values in the face of rising sea levels from global climate change.

The zones represented in this report reinforce the argument of sustainable development which integrates infrastructure and conventional real estate into an integrated development model. By testing the notions and feasibility of hyper density, this report raises the provocation of a highly urbanized way of life that is financially, socially and environmentally sustainable. Hyper density can be environmentally sustainable due to production and operating efficiencies and economies of scale. Hyper density can be more socially sustainable because diversity in household composition, household income, housing unit size and housing tenure reinforces the requisite diverse population reflected in mature urban settlements. Finally, these exercises promote financially sustainability to the extent that value capture instrumentation reinforced by measurement techniques applied in this report could help facilitate an investment in infrastructure that reflects a more equitable burden between users and benefactors. However, the goals of this project are much more humble. The aim has been to develop a series of tools and corresponding workflows that iteratively automates many of the analytical processes found in interdisciplinary design and development exercises. In this case, scenario planning for future households is just one of an untold number of applications available for management of the built environment.

It should be acknowledged that households will evolve, especially in the face of an aging society. The amount of space each future resident of NYC will take up in terms of their daily commuting, sleeping, and working patterns is anyone's guess. The trends in favor of denser spaces which are more aligned with global urban standards are undeniable. This report is not about projecting a future, as much as it is about simulating a scenario. The scenarios presented in this report seek to understand what it would look like and how much it would cost to house the next one million New Yorkers. By testing the imposition of a large fraction of the next one million new New Yorkers, this report seeks to advance the notion that hyper density in select areas of NYC could not only be feasible but have long-term positive impacts ranging from the increased global competitiveness to a higher quality of life for the next generation of New Yorkers.

BIBLIOGRAPHY

Achten, Henri, *Experiment Design Methods: A Review*, 7 INT.'L J. OF ARCHITECTURAL COMPUTING 4, 505 (2010).

Atkinson-Palombo, C., *Comparing the Capitalization Benefits of Light Rail Transit and Overlay Zoning for Single Family Houses and Condos by Neighborhood Type in Metropolitan Phoenix*, 47 URBAN STUDIES 2409-2426 (2010).

Baum-Snow, N. and Kahn, M., *The Effects of New Public Projects to Expand Urban Rail Transit*, 77 J. OF PUBLIC ECONOMICS 241-263 (2000).

Bean, Vicki, *Impact Fees and Housing Affordability*, 8 CITYSCAPE 1, 139 (2005).

Beyler, Blinder & Belle Architects & Planners, *Master Plan: Caemmerer West Side Yard* (1989).

Berghauser Pont, Meta and Haupt, Per, SPACEMATRIX: SPACE, DENSITY AND URBAN Form (NAI Publishers 2010).

Buckhurst, Fish, Hutton, Katz. *The Future of the Piers: Planning and Designation for Brooklyn Piers 1-6* (1987).

The Brookings Institution: Metropolitan Policy Program, *Counting for Dollars: New York, NY-NJ-PA* (2008).

Bureau of Labor Statistics, New York-New Jersey Information Office, *New York City/New York State: State and Area Employment, Hours and Earnings (Non-Farm)*(2012).

Carr, Lucas, et. al, *Validation of Walk Score for Estimating Access to Walkable Amenities*, 45 BR. J. SPORTS MED 1144-1148 (2011).

Cervero, R. and Duncan, M., *Transit's Valued-Added Effects: Light and Commuter Rail Services and Commercial Land Values*, Transportation Research Record, 1805, 8-15 (2002).

Citizens Housing & Planning Council, *Making Room* (2011).

Cox, Wendell, *The Accelerating Suburbanization of New York*, NEW GEOGRAPHY (March 29, 2011).

Cross, Nigel, ENGINEERING DESIGN METHODS: STRATEGIES FOR PRODUCT DESIGN (Wiley 2000).

Delaney, Charles J. and Smith, Marc T., *Impact Fees and the Price of New Housing: An Empirical Study, AREUAE Journal* 17: 41–54 (1989).

Delaney, Charles J. and Smith, Marc T., *Pricing Implications of Development Exactions on Existing Housing Stock, Growth and Change* 20: 1–12 (1989).

Dresch, Marla and Sheffrin, Steven M., *Who Pays for Development Fees and Exactions?* San Francisco: Public Policy Institute of California (1997).

Duncan, Dustin T., et. al, *Validation of Walk Score® for Estimating Neighborhood Walkability: An Analysis for Four US Metropolitan Areas*, 8 INT. J. ENVIRON. RES. PUBLIC HEALTH 4160-4179 (2011).

Duncan, M., *The Impact of Transit-Oriented Development on Housing Prices in San Diego, CA.*, 48 URBAN STUDIES 101-127 (2011).

The Economist, *Hot Spots: Benchmarking Global City Competitiveness*, Economist Intelligence Unit (2012).

Empire State Development Corporation, *Atlantic Yards Land Use Improvements and Civic Project: Modified General Project Plan* (2009).

Empire State Development Corporation, *Urban Renewal Area and Historical District Boundaries* (1996).

Fowler, Glenn, Renewal Raises Brooklyn Hopes; $250-Million Plan Advanced for Atlantic Terminal Area, N.Y. TIMES (June 24, 1968).

Frampton, Kenneth, *The Generic Street as a Continuous Built Form*, in ON STREETS (MIT Press 1986).

Furman Center for Real Estate and Urban Policy, New York University, *State of the City's Housing & Neighborhoods* (2001-2011).

Governor Andrew M. Cuomo Press Office, *Governor Cuomo Holds Meeting with New York's Congressional Delegation, Mayor Bloomberg and Regional County Executives to Review Damage Assessment for the State in the Wake of Hurricane Sandy*, Press Release (November 26, 2012).

Gruzen & Partners &The Lefrank Organization, *A Feasibility Study for the Multiple Use of Air-Rights Over the Sunnyside Yards* (1975).

The Gruzen Partnership, *Hunters Point: Waterfront Development* (1986).

Harlem Urban Development Corporation. *10 year Development Proposal: HUDC Task Force Preliminary Report* (1973).

Harris, Elizabeth A., *Decades-Old Housing 'Emergency' Continues, and So Does Rent Regulation*, N.Y. TIMES (March 26, 2012).

Hart, Krivatsy & Stubee, *Corona East-Elmhurst Development Program* (1970).

Hillsborough County Planning Commission, Fiscal Impact Estimates of Land Development (FIELD)(2009)(available at http://www.tpcfieldmodel.org/FIELD)(last accessed October 10, 2012).

Hess, D.B. and Almeida, T.M., *Impact of Proximity to Light Rail Transit on Station-area Property Values in Buffalo, New York*, 44 URBAN STUDIES 1041-1068 (2007).

Ihlanfeldt, Keith and Shaughnessy, Timothy M., *An Empirical Investigation of the Effects of Impact Fees on Housing and Land Markets*, 34 REGIONAL SCIENCE AND URBAN ECONOMICS 639–661 (2004).

Ingram, Gregory K. and Ho, Yu-Hung, eds., VALUE CAPTURE AND LAND POLICIES (Lincoln Institute of Land Policy 2011).

Jacobs, Allen B., GREAT STREETS (MIT Press 2001).

Jacobs, Allen B., MacDonald, Elizabeth and Rofe, Yodan, THE BOULEVARD BOOK: HISTORY, EVOLUTION, DESIGN OF MULTIWAY BOULEVARDS (MIT Press 2003).

Jones, John Chris, DESIGN METHODS: SEEDS OF HUMAN FUTURES (Wiley 1981).

Keenan, Barnard V., *A Perspective: New York Communities and Impact Fees*, 7 PACE ENVT'L. L. REV. 2, 329 (1990).

King, David A. and Keenan, Jesse M., *Understanding the Role of Parking Lots in Urban Redevelopment*, Center for Urban Real Estate, Columbia University (July 2012).

Kotval, Zenia and Mullin, John, *Fiscal Impact Analysis: Methods, Cases and Intellectual Debate*, Lincoln Land Institute (September 2006).

Krause, Andy L. and Bitter, Christopher, *Spatial Econometrics, Land Values and Sustainability: Trends in Real Estate Valuation Research*, CITIES (July 2012).

Lee, Moon Wha, *Selected Initial Finding of the 2011 New York City Housing and Vacancy Survey*, New York City Department of Housing Preservation and Development (February 9, 2012).

Levy, Charles, Sissons, Andrew and Holloway, Charlotte, *A Plan for Growth in the Knowledge Economy (U.K.)*, A Knowledge Economy Programmer Paper, The Work Foundation (June 2011).

Litman, Todd, *Where We Want to Be: Home Location Preferences and Their Implications for Smart Growth*, Victoria Transport Policy Institute (July 26, 2012).

Lwin, Ko Ko and Murayama, Yuki, *Modeling of Urban Green Space Walkability: Eco-friendly Walk Score Calculator*, 35 COMPUTERS, ENVIRONMENT AND URBAN SYSTEMS 408-420 (2011).

McMahon, E.J. and Barro, Josh, *New York's Exploding Pension Costs*, Empire Center for New York State Policy, SR8-11 (2010).

Madanipour, Ali, KNOWLEDGE ECONOMY AND THE CITY: SPACES OF KNOWLEDGE (Taylor & Francis Group 2011).

Metropolitan Transportation Council, *A Shared Vision for Shared Future: Regional Transportation Plan* (2010).

Mooney, Jake, Rezoning Clears Way for 'Small City' in the Bronx, N.Y. TIMES (July 24, 2012).

The Mori Memorial Foundation, *Global Power City Index*, Institute for Urban Strategies (2011).

National Association of Realtors, *Cities with the Largest Average Home Sizes*, REALTOR MAGAZINE (January 03, 2012).

New York Committee on Slum Clearance. *Morningside Manhattanville: Slum Clearance Plan Under Title I of the Housing Act of 1949* (1951).

New York Committee on Slum Clearance, *Fort Greene slum clearance plan under Title I of the Housing Act of 1949* (1952).

New York Committee on Slum Clearance, *Seward Park Project* (1956).

New York Committee on Slum Clearance, *Title I Progress: Quarterly Report on Slum Clearance Project* (1960).

NYC Department of Housing Preservation and Development, *Distribution of Occupied and Vacant Available Units by Building Size*, New York City Housing and Vacancy Survey (2008).

NYC New York City Department of Housing Preservation & Development, *Willets Point Urban Renewal Area* (2008).

NYC Department of City Planning. *Red Hook Redevelopment Plan & Program* (1970).

NYC Department of City Planning: South Bronx Community Planning Unit, *Strengthening Hunts Point* (1974).

NYC Department of City Planning: South Bronx Community Planning Unit, *A Proposal for Change: Interim Proposals for Bronx Community Planning District 3* (1975).

NYC Department of City Planning, *Action Program for South Brooklyn Waterfront and Columbia Street* (1978).

NYC Department of City Planning, *Stapleton: A Commercial Revitalization Plan* (1979).

NYC Department of City Planning, *The Convention Center Area: Recommendations for Land Use, Zoning, and Development* (1984).

NYC Department of City Planning, *Grand Concourse Special Zoning District Proposal* (1986).

NYC Department of City Planning, *Elmhurst / Corona, Queens: A Planning Proposal* (1989).

NYC Department of City Planning, *Hunts Point Peninsula Planning Recommendations* (1989).

NYC Department of City Planning. *Rego Park, Queens: A Planning Proposal* (1989).

NYC Department of City Planning, *Plan for Brooklyn Waterfront* (1992).

NYC Department of City Planning, *Stapleton: A Commercial Revitalization Plan* (1992).

NYC Department of City Planning, *Downtown Flushing Plan* (1993).

NYC Department of City Planning, *The Plan for Lower Manhattan* (1993).

NYC Department of City Planning, *Plan for the Brooklyn Waterfront: New York City Comprehensive Waterfront Plan* (1994).

NYC Department of City Planning, *Red Hook: A Plan for Community Regeneration* (1996).

NYC Department of City Planning, *Lower Manhattan Plan* (1998).

NYC Department of City Planning, *Long Island City Rezoning* (2004).

NYC Department of City Planning, *Port Morris/Bruckner Boulevard Rezoning* (2005).

NYC Department of City Planning, *New York City Population Projections Age/Sex & Borough 2000-2030 Report* (2006).

NYC Department of City Planning, *Stapleton Waterfront Rezoning* (2006).

NYC Department of City Planning, *125th Street Unzoning Plan* (2007).

NYC Department of City Planning, *Hunters Point South Redevelopment Plan* (2007).

NYC Department of City Planning, *Bronx Borough Office, Special Hunts Point District Plan* (2008).

NYC Department of City Planning, *Lower Concourse Rezoning* (2009).

NYC Department of City Planning, *East River Waterfront Esplanade* (2011).

NYC Department of City Planning, *Hudson Yards* (Updated 2012).

NYC Department of City Planning, *Population: 2010 Census Challenge* (April 1, 2012).

NYC Economic Development Corporation & Department of City Planning, *Downtown Brooklyn* (2004).

NYC Economic Development Corporation & Department of Housing Preservation and Development, *Seward Park Mixed-Use Development Project* (2012).

NYC Economic Development Corporation, *Stapleton Waterfront Development Plan* (2012).

NYC Planning Commission, *Master Plan of Brooklyn Civic Center & Downtown Area: Master Plan of Desirable Building Zone Districts for Brooklyn Civic Center & Downtown Area* (1945).

NYC Planning Commission, *Brooklyn Heights Historic District* (1964).

NYC Planning Commission, *Lower Manhattan Plan* (1966).

New York State Department of Labor, *Press Release* (November 15, 2012).

New York World's Fair Commission, *World Fair Master Plan* (1939).

Nelson, Arthur C., et al., *Price Effects of Road and Other Impact Fees on Urban Land*, TRANSPORTATION RESEARCH RECORD 1305: 36–41 (1992).

Nelson, Arthur C., *Reforming Infrastructure Financing in a Fiscally Constrained World*, Metropolitan Research Center, University of Utah (2010).

Nicholas, James C., Nelson, Arthur C. & Juergensmeyer, Julian C., A PRACTITIONER'S GUIDE TO DEVELOPMENT IMPACT FEES (American Planning Association 1991).

Office of the Borough President of Queens. *Advancing a Local and Regional Transportation Network: A Proposal to Coordinate Major Rail Systems in the Borough of Queens* (1991).

Office of Downtown Brooklyn Development and the Office of the Mayor, *Atlantic Avenue Special Zoning District* (1974).

The Parks Council, *Creating Public Access to the Brooklyn Waterfront* (1990).

Plimmer, Frances and McGill, Greg, *Land Value Taxation: Betterment Taxation in England and the Potential for Change*, Paper Presented at International Federation of Surveyors (FIG) Working Week (April 2003).

Project for Public Spaces, Inc., *125th Street Study* (1977).

Raymond & May Associates. *Vest pocket housing in Bedford-Stuyvesant : A Summary Report to the Community and City on Some of the First Steps in New York's Model Cities Program* (1968).

Roberts, Sam, *New York Led Country in Population Growth Since 2010 Census*, N.Y. TIMES (June 28, 2012).

Rushing, Amy S., Kneifel, Joshua D. and Lippiatt, Barbara C., *Energy Price Indices and Discount Factors for Life-Cycle Cost Analysis- 2011*, U.S. Department of Energy Federal Energy Management Program, NSTIR-85-3273-26 (September 11, 2011).

Sandroni, Paulo Henrique, *Recent Experience with Land Value Capture in São Paulo, Brazil*, Land Lines (Lincoln Institute of Land Policy July 2011).

Schwartz, Eduardo and Torous, Walter N., *Commercial Office Space: Tests of Real Options Model with Competitive Interactions*, Paper Presented at the American Finance Association Annual Meeting (2004).

Signature Urban Properties, LLC, *West Farms Road Redevelopment Plan* (2012).

Silverstien Properties, Inc. and Port Authority of New York & New Jersey, *Master Plan for Memorial and New World Trade Center* (2007).

Singell, Larry D. and Lillydahl, Jane H., *Housing Impact Fees*, 66 LAND ECONOMICS 1, 82–92 (1990).

Skaburskis, Andrejs and Qadeer, Mohammad, *An Empirical Estimation of the Price Effects of Development Impact Fees*, 29 URBAN STUDIES 653–667 (1992).

Southern Bronx River Watershed Alliance, Alternatives 1E and 2E (July 2012)(available at http://www.southbronxvision.org/oakpoint.html)(last accessed October 2012).

Starwood Capital Group and Toll Brothers City Living©, *Pier 1 Development Plan* (2012).

Walmsley & Company, *The North Shore Esplanade* (1979).

Wheaton, William C., Real Estate *"Cycles": Some Fundamentals*, 2 REAL ESTATE ECONOMICS 27, 209 (1999).

APPENDIX

APPENDIX TABLE 1: DEVELOPMENT INDEX WEIGHTING BY SUB-CATEGORY

Sub-Category	Notes	Rank
If Historic District or Landmark, then:		X*

ZONING		
1. Mixed Manufacturing	M1-1/R-5 to M1-6/R10	5
2. Manufacturing	M1-1 to M3-2	4
3. Commercial	C1-6 to C8-4	3
4. Residential	R1-1 to R10H	1
5. Parks	PARK or PARKNY	0

BUILDING CLASS		
1. E (Warehouses)	exclude E6 (Ratio 0 to 1)	5
2. V (Not-Zoned Resi)		5
2. F (Industrial Bldgs.)		5
3. K1 , K2, K3**		4
3. G (Garage & Gas Station)	except G0 (Ratio 1 to 1)	4
3. H (Hotels)	except H2 (Ratio 1 to 1)	3
4. L (Loft Bldgs.)		3
3. B (Two Family Dwellings)		2
4. C (Walk Up Apartments)		2
6. K (Store Bldgs.)		1
5. M (Religious Bldgs.)		1
5. D (Elevator Apartments)		1
6. A (One Family Dwellings)		1
7. J (Theaters)		1
8. I (Hospitals & Health)		1
9. N (Asylums & Homes)		1
10. O (Office Bldgs.)		1
11. K (Store Bldgs.)	except K1-3	1
12. R,S**		1
13. Q, P, T, U, W, Y, Z**		0

LAND USE CODE (DCP)		
1. 11 (Vacant Land)		5
2. 10 (Parking Facilities)		4
3. 6 (Industrial & Manu-facturing)		3
4. 5 (Commercial & Office Bldgs.)		2
5. 1, 2 (One-, Two- & Multi-Family Walk-up)		2
6. 3 (Family Elevator Bldgs.)		1
7. 7,8,9**		0

YEAR BUILT		
1. 1920s-1940s		5
2. 1960s-1970s		4
3. 1950s		4
3. 1980s		3
4. 1990s-2000s		1
5. XXXX -1910s		1

LOT TYPE**		
1. 0 (Mixed or Unknown)	i.e., Code 0	1
2. 1 (Block Assemblage)		4
3. 2 (Waterfront)		3
4. 3 (Corner)		5
5. 4 (Through)		4
6. 5 (Inside)		2
7. 6 (Interior Lot)		2
8. 7 (Island Lot)		1
9. 8 (Alley Lot)		1
10. 9 (Submerged Land Lot)		1
12. R,S		1
13. Q, P, T, U, W, Y, Z		0

* X = Override Exclusion

** Refer to http://www.nyc.gov/html/dcp/html/bytes/meta_mappluto.shtml

APPENDIX TABLE 2:
LIST OF REAL ESTATE
ASSUMPTIONS / OUTPUTS

ASSUMPTIONS	
Discount Rate (NPV)	15.00%
Capital Discount Rate	3.00%
Rent Inflation	3.00%
Expense Inflation	4.00%
Soft Costs	30.00%
Hard Costs	$250 to $700 Per Sq. Ft.
Weighted Averge Cost of Capital (WACC)	7.00%
Permant Debt Term	X^T Months
Permant Debt Type	Amortized
Loan-to-Value (LTV)	80.00%
Loan-to-Cost (LTC)	65.00%
Vacancy / Credit Loss	10.00%
Residential Operating Expenses	20.00%
Retail Operating Expenses	15.00%
Capital Expenses	5.00%
Capitalization Rates (Sale)	4.50% to 8.00%
Transaction Costs (Sale)	10.00%
Residential Loss Factor	20.00%
Retail Loss Factor	15.00%
Residential Sales Price	$800 to $4,000 Per Sq. Ft.
Residential Rental Price	$22 to $65 Per Sq. Ft.
Office Rent	$45 to $120
Retail Rent	$100 to $2,200
OUTPUTS	
Net Operating Income (NOI)	
Net Present Value (NPV) @ X^T Discount Rate	
Debt Service	
Pre-tax Cash Flow	
Cash-on-Cash	
Levered and Unlevered Internal Rate of Return (IRR) @ X^T	
Levered and Unlevered Return on Equity (ROE) @ X^T	

APPENDIX TABLE 3:
EXPANDED HOUSEHOLD COMPOSITION / SPACE ALLOCATION PROJECTIONS

	HOUSEHOLD COMPOSITION	HOUSEHOLD / FAMILY SIZE	AVERAGE SIZE PER PERSON	AVERAGE SIZE OF UNIT
17%	Nuclear Family	3.32	450	1,494
22%	Single / Alone	1.00	450	450
10%	Single Under-Occupy (2br or larger)	1.00	900	900
6%	Shared (unrelated roommates)	2.59	450	1,166
20%	Shared (w/family)	3.32	450	1,494
17%	Couples with no children	2.00	450	900
8%	Single Parents	3.32	450	1,494
100%	Total Households			
502	Average Sq. Ft. Per Person			
1,301	Average Sq. Ft. Per Household			
2.59	Average Household Size			

HOUSEHOLDS						
	NYC TOTAL	BKY	QNS	BRX	SI	MN
Nuclear Family	15,098	4,638	4,116	2,549	862	2,933
Single / Alone	19,539	6,002	5,327	3,299	1,115	3,796
Single Under-Occupy	8,881	2,728	2,421	1,499	507	1,726
Shared (unrelated roommates)	5,329	1,637	1,453	900	304	1,035
Shared (w/family)	17,762	5,456	4,843	2,999	1,014	3,451
Couples with no children	15,098	4,638	4,116	2,549	862	2,933
Single Parents	7,105	2,182	1,937	1,200	405	1,380
Total Households	88,812	27,281	24,213	14,994	5,068	17,256

SQUARE FOOTAGE						
	NYC TOTAL	BKY	QNS	BRX	SI	MN
Nuclear Family	22,556,355	6,928,789	6,149,643	3,808,227	1,287,100	4,382,596
Single / Alone	8,792,342	2,700,804	2,397,097	1,484,426	501,704	1,708,312
Single Under-Occupy	7,993,039	2,455,276	2,179,179	1,349,478	456,095	1,553,011
Shared (unrelated roommates)	6,210,591	1,907,749	1,693,222	1,048,545	354,386	1,206,689
Shared (w/family)	26,536,888	8,151,516	7,234,875	4,480,267	1,514,235	5,155,995
Couples with no children	13,588,166	4,173,969	3,704,605	2,294,113	775,361	2,640,118
Single Parents	10,614,755	3,260,606	2,893,950	1,792,107	605,694	2,062,398
Total Households	92,292,136	29,578,709	26,252,571	16,257,163	5,494,574	18,709,118

APPENDIX TABLE 4: MODEL PROJECTED DISTRIBUTION (w/ MEGAPROJECTS)

	RESIDENTIAL SQ. FT.	FOR SALE	RENTAL	RETAIL SQ. FT.	OFFICE SQ. FT.	ANNUAL GROWTH*	TOTAL GROWTH
MANHATTAN							
125th St	4,523,180	1,415,755	3,107,425	450,206	297,221	188,236	5,270,607
Lower Manhattan (WTC)	11,814,261	3,697,864	8,116,397	1,175,909	776,322	491,660	13,766,492
Seward Park	7,414,500	2,320,739	5,093,762	858,495	501,722	313,383	8,774,717
West Side	17,500,000	5,477,500	12,022,500	1,000,000	24,000,000	1,517,857	42,500,000
Total(s)	41,251,942	12,911,858	28,340,084	3,484,610	25,575,265	2,511,136	70,311,816
QUEENS							
Long Island City/Sunny Side	19,861,114	6,216,529	13,644,585	442,086	1,041,732	762,319	21,344,932
Queens Blvd	13,041,457	4,081,976	8,959,481	311,533	1,028,354	513,619	14,381,345
Willet's Point	5,500,000	1,721,500	3,778,500	1,400,000	500,000	264,286	7,400,000
Total(s)	38,402,571	12,020,005	26,382,566	2,153,619	2,570,087	1,540,224	43,126,277
BROOKLYN							
Atlantic Ave/Fulton St	10,668,756	3,339,321	7,329,435	212,379	298,499	399,273	11,179,633
Atlantic Yards	6,400,000	2,003,200	4,396,800	247,000	336,000	249,393	6,983,000
Brooklyn Waterfront	4,740,047	1,483,635	3,256,413	94,358	289,277	182,989	5,123,683
Downtown Brooklyn	9,739,918	3,048,594	6,691,324	193,889	963,478	389,189	10,897,285
Red Hook	10,345,730	3,238,213	7,107,516	205,948	781,108	404,742	11,332,786
Total(s)	41,894,451	13,112,963	28,781,488	953,574	2,668,362	1,625,585	45,516,387
BRONX							
Sheridan Expressway	10,514,984	3,291,190	7,223,794	209,318	690,946	407,687	11,415,247
South Concourse	8,993,612	2,815,001	6,178,611	179,032	590,976	348,701	9,763,620
Total(s)	19,508,596	6,106,190	13,402,405	388,350	1,281,922	756,388	21,178,867
STATEN ISLAND							
St George/Stapleton	6,593,489	2,063,762	4,529,727	105,003	433,262	254,706	7,131,755
Total(s)	6,593,489	2,063,762	4,529,727	105,003	433,262	254,706	7,131,755
TOTAL	147,651,049	46,214,778	101,436,270	7,085,156	32,528,898	6,688,039	187,265,102

* Straightline Distribution

APPENDIX TABLE 5: MODEL PROJECTED DISTRIBUTION (w/o MEGAPROJECTS)

	RESIDENTIAL SQ. FT.	FOR SALE	RENTAL	RETAIL SQ. FT.	OFFICE SQ. FT.	ANNUAL GROWTH*	TOTAL GROWTH
MANHATTAN							
125th St	4,523,180	1,415,755	3,107,425	450,206	297,221	188,236	5,270,607
Lower Manhattan (WTC)	11,814,261	3,697,864	8,116,397	1,175,909	776,322	491,660	13,766,492
Seward Park	6,113,500	1,913,526	4,199,975	608,495	401,722	254,418	7,123,717
West Side	0	0	0	0	0	0	0
Total(s)	22,450,942	7,027,145	15,423,797	2,234,610	1,475,265	934,315	26,160,816
QUEENS							
Long Island City/Sunny Side	13,211,114	4,135,079	9,076,035	315,586	1,041,732	520,301	14,568,432
Queens Blvd	13,041,457	4,081,976	8,959,481	311,533	1,028,354	513,619	14,381,345
Willet's Point	0	0	0	0	0	0	0
Total(s)	26,252,571	8,217,055	18,035,516	627,119	2,070,087	1,033,921	28,949,777
BROOKLYN							
Atlantic Ave/Fulton St	10,668,756	3,339,321	7,329,435	212,379	298,499	399,273	11,179,633
Atlantic Yards	0	0	0	0	0	0	0
Brooklyn Waterfront	4,740,047	1,483,635	3,256,413	94,358	289,277	182,989	5,123,683
Downtown Brooklyn	9,739,918	3,048,594	6,691,324	193,889	963,478	389,189	10,897,285
Red Hook	10,345,730	3,238,213	7,107,516	205,948	781,108	404,742	11,332,786
Total(s)	35,494,451	11,109,763	24,384,688	706,574	2,332,362	1,376,192	38,533,387
BRONX							
Sheridan Expressway	10,514,984	3,291,190	7,223,794	209,318	690,946	407,687	11,415,247
South Concourse	8,993,612	2,815,001	6,178,611	179,032	590,976	348,701	9,763,620
Total(s)	19,508,596	6,106,190	13,402,405	388,350	1,281,922	756,388	21,178,867
STATEN ISLAND							
St George/Stapleton	6,593,489	2,063,762	4,529,727	105,003	433,262	254,706	7,131,755
Total(s)	6,593,489	2,063,762	4,529,727	105,003	433,262	254,706	7,131,755
TOTAL	110,300,049	34,523,915	75,776,133	4,061,656	7,592,898	4,355,522	121,954,602

* Straightline Distribution

APPENDIX TABLE 6: PROJECTED TOTAL SPACE ALLOCATIONS (w/ MEGAPROJECTS)

	RESI SQ. FT.	UNITS	POPULATION	RETAIL SQ. FT.	OFFICE SQ. FT.	TOTAL SQ. FT.
Westside	17,500,000	13,451	34,839	1,000,000	24,000,000	42,500,000
Willets Point	5,500,000	4,228	10,949	1,400,000	500,000	7,400,000
Atlantic Yards	6,400,000	4,919	12,741	247,000	336,000	6,983,000
Seward Park	1,301,000	1,000	2,590	250,000	100,000	1,651,000
Hunters Point	6,650,000	6,650	17,224	126,500	0	6,776,500
TOTAL	37,351,000	30,248	78,342	3,023,500	24,936,000	65,310,500
Total + Projected	147,651,049	113,490	293,940	7,085,156	24,936,000	187,265,102

APPENDIX TABLE 7: MEASURED TAX RELATED IMPACTS & ASSUMPTIONS

PROPERTY TAX
Market Value
Assessed Value
Annual Tax (YOS)

CONSTRUCTION RELATED REVENUE
Construction Cost
Estimated Materials Taxable Base ($)

SALES & MISC. TAX
Retail Sales Tax (%)
Retail Sales Per Resident
Retail Sales By Household Composition & Income
Retail Sales (PSF)
Total Annual Retail Sales
Total Sales Tax
(%) of Income Subject to Sales Tax
Per Capita Income
Total Resident Wages (After-Tax, AMI)
Total Sales Tax (Residents)
Hotel Room Occupancy Tax (Rate)
NYC ADR
Hotel Room Occupancy Tax
Commercial Rent Tax (CRT) Rate
Discount to Rent (CRT)
Avg. Commercial Lease PSF (CRT)
Taxable Base (CRT)
Total CRT

EMPLOYMENT TAXES
Area Median Income (AMI)(2011)
State Tax Rate
City Tax Rate
Avg. Weekly Wage (Construction)
Annualized Wage (Construction)
Aggregate Wages (Construction)
State Tax (Construction)
City Tax (Construction)
Avg. Weekly Wage (Profession/Business Services)
Annualized Wage (Profession/Business Services)
Aggregate Wages (Professional/Business Services)

EMPLOYMENT TAXES (CONT.)
State Tax (Professional/Business Services)
City Tax (Professional/Business Services)
Retail Weekly Wage (Retail)
Annualized Wage (Retail)
Aggregate Wages (Retail)
State Tax (Retail)
City Tax (Retail)
Avg. Weekly Wage (Other)
Annualized Wage (Other)
Aggregate Wages (Other)
State Tax (Other)
City Tax (Other)
Total State Tax (Reoccuring)
Total City Tax (Reoccuring)
Total Wages (Reoccuring)
Avg. Wage per Employee (Reoccuring)
Avg. Wage (% of AMI) (Reoccuring)

TOTAL CITY & STATE TAX REVENUE (REOCCURING)
Property
Sales
Employment
Total

PUBLIC + PRIVATE NET IMPACT
Imputed Infrastructure Cost (Reoccuring)
Total City Revenues
Total Public Revenues
Cost / City Income
Cost / Public Income
Estimated Public Infrastructure Cost (Sum of Simulations)
Years of Impact Fee Amortization (I = 10 yrs)
Years of Impact Fee Amortization (II = 20 yrs)
Impact Fee (Noreoccuring) (I)
Impact Fee (Nonreoccuring) (II)
Impact Fee (Reoccuring & Nonreoccuring) (I)
Impact Fee (Reoccuring & Nonreoccuring) (II)
Impact Fee (% of Cost) (I)
Impact Fee (% of Cost) (II)

APPENDIX TABLE 8:
URBAN BENCHMARKING CRITERIA

POPULATION DENSITY	# Residents / 5,000ft = SUM[(Residential Area of each lot from GIS) * (Residential Area Loss Factor) * (average Residential Area per Person)] / 5,000ft
JOB DENSITY	# Employees / 5,000ft = SUM[(Office/Retail/Industrial Area of each lot from GIS) * (Office/Retail/Industrial Area Loss Factor) * (Average Office/Retail/Industrial Area per Person)] / 5,000ft
AVERAGE FAR	MEAN value of [FAR value from each lot from GIS]
PEDESTRIAN ACCESS	(Each Block Area) * (Average Walk Time from Block to Subway Stops)
SUBWAY STOPS/0.5 MI	[0.5 mile Square Area/(Zone Study Area)] * (number of Subway Stops in Zone Study Area)
BUS STOPS / 0.5 MI	[0.5 mile Square Area/(Zone Study Area)] * (number of bus Stops in Zone Study Area)
BIKE LANES / 5000 FT	(Total Bike Lane Length in Zone) / Overall Study Area * 5,000 ft
AVERAGE SKY EXPOSURE (PLAZAS)	MEAN value of [(Number of 3d Rays from Each Interval Points on Plaza Not Obstructed by Buildings) / (Total number of 3d rays from each interval points)]
AVERAGE SKY EXPOSURE (STREETS)	MEAN value of [(Number of 3d Rays from Each Interval Points on Street Not Obstructed by Buildings) / (Total Number of 3d Rays from Each Interval Points)]
AVERAGE STREET WIDTH	MEAN value of (Width of Street from Each Intersection Point)
AVERAGE INTERSECTION DISTANCE	MEAN value of (Distance from Street Intersection Point to Closest Intersection Point)
INTERSECTIONS/0.5 MI	[0.5 mile Square Area / (ZoneStudy Area)] * (number of Intersections in Overall Study Area)
AVERAGE BLOCK PERIMETER	MEAN value of [(Perimeter Length of Each Block in Study Area)]
AVERAGE STREET WALL %	SUM[(Length Along Each Block with Building Façade) / (Perimeter of Entire Block)]
COVERAGE RATIO	SUM(Area of Each Building Footprints) / SUM(Area of Each Block Size)
OPEN SPACE RATIO	[(Overall Site Area)-SUM(Area of Each Building Footprint)] / Overall Site Area
PUBLIC SPACE %	SUM(Area of Public Spaces in Zone) / Overall Study Area
RETAIL %	(Total Retail Area from GIS of Entire Site) / (Total Building Area from GIS of Entire Site)

APPENDIX TABLE 9:
URBAN BENCHMARKING INDICES

DENSITY	(PD Weight value: 0.20) * (Population Density Score) + (JD Weight Value: 0.15) * (Job Density Score) + + (FAR Weight Value: 0.35) * (FAR Score) + (CR Weight Value: 0.30) * (Coverage Ratio Score)
WALK SCORE (Note: Measuring travel distance along streets with walk speed of 1.4 M/S)	(Subway Score) * (Subway Weight Value : 0.05) + (Bus Score) * (Bus Weight Value : 0.10) + (Bike Score) * (Bike Weight Value: 0.05) + (# Intersections Score) * (Intersections Weight Value: 0.10) + (Street Sky Exposure Score)*(SSE Weight Value: 0.20) + (Pedestrian Access Score of only Walk times under 10)*(PA Weight Value: 0.20) + (Street Width Scores of only Street widths exceeding 40) * (SW Weight: 0.15) + (Intersection Distance Scores of only Distances exceeding 300) * (ID Weight: 0.05) + (Block Size Scores of only Blocks exceeding 1320) * (BS Weight: 0.05) + (Street Wall Scores only exceeding 20%) * (SW Weight: 0.05)
PUBLIC SPACE	(Plaza Sky Exposure Score) * (PSE Weight Value: 0.20) + (Street Sky Exposure Score) * (SSE Weight Value: 0.20) + (Open Space Score) * (OS Weight Value: 0.20) + (Public Space Score) * (PS Weight Value: 0.25) + (Retail Score)*(Retail Weight: 0.15)

APPENDIX MAP 1:
MANHATTAN SAMPLE CATCHMENT AREAS FOR
URBAN BENCHMARKING AVERAGE COMPARISONS

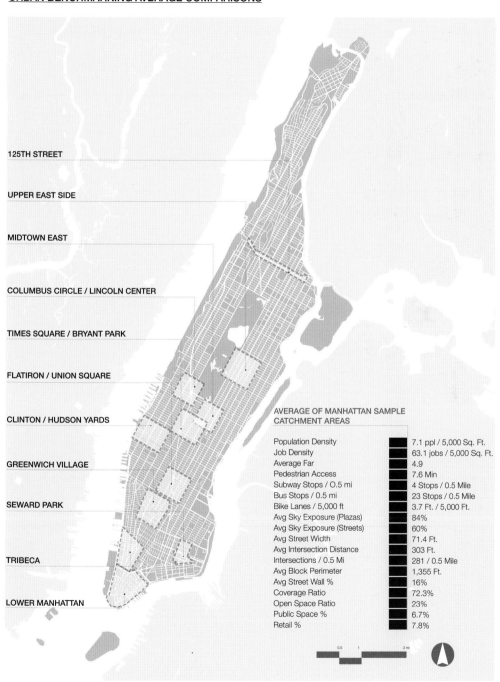

125TH STREET

UPPER EAST SIDE

MIDTOWN EAST

COLUMBUS CIRCLE / LINCOLN CENTER

TIMES SQUARE / BRYANT PARK

FLATIRON / UNION SQUARE

CLINTON / HUDSON YARDS

GREENWICH VILLAGE

SEWARD PARK

TRIBECA

LOWER MANHATTAN

AVERAGE OF MANHATTAN SAMPLE
CATCHMENT AREAS

Population Density	7.1 ppl / 5,000 Sq. Ft.
Job Density	63.1 jobs / 5,000 Sq. Ft.
Average Far	4.9
Pedestrian Access	7.6 Min
Subway Stops / 0.5 mi	4 Stops / 0.5 Mile
Bus Stops / 0.5 mi	23 Stops / 0.5 Mile
Bike Lanes / 5,000 ft	3.7 Ft. / 5,000 Ft.
Avg Sky Exposure (Plazas)	84%
Avg Sky Exposure (Streets)	60%
Avg Street Width	71.4 Ft.
Avg Intersection Distance	303 Ft.
Intersections / 0.5 Mi	281 / 0.5 Mile
Avg Block Perimeter	1,355 Ft.
Avg Street Wall %	16%
Coverage Ratio	72.3%
Open Space Ratio	23%
Public Space %	6.7%
Retail %	7.8%